But He'll Change

But He'll Change

Ending the Thinking
That Keeps You in Abusive Relationships

Joanna V. Hunter

HAZELDEN®

Hazelden
Center City, Minnesota 55012
hazelden.org

Library of Congress Cataloging-in-Publication Data

Hunter, Joanna V., 1949–
   But he'll change : ending the thinking that keeps you in abusive relationships / Joanna V. Hunter.
      p. cm.
   Includes bibliographical references.
   ISBN 978-1-59285-818-7 (softcover)
   1. Abused women—Psychology. 2. Intimate partner violence—Prevention.
   3. Family violence—Prevention. 4. Abusive men. I. Title.
   HV6626.H86 2010
   362.82'92—dc22
                                                    2009042701

Editor's note
While the stories and lives shared in this book are true, names and other identifying information have been changed to provide anonymity.
   This publication is not intended as a substitute for the advice of health care professionals.

14 13 12 11 10   1 2 3 4 5 6

Cover design by Theresa Gedig
Interior design and typesetting by Madeline Berglund

To my husband,
who by word and action
reminds me every day
that I am loved and cherished.

And to those who surrounded me and
supported me as I healed.

CONTENTS

Chapter 1

Chapter 2

Chapter 3

Chapter 4

Chapter 5

Chapter 6

Chapter 7

Chapter 8

Appendix A

Appendix B

EDITOR'S NOTE

Interviews with domestic abuse experts Darald Hanusa, Ph.D., L.C.S.W., Jennifer Parker, M.S.S.W., L.C.S.W., Eve Lipchik, M.S.W., Robert D. Enright, Ph.D., and Ann Brickson, M.S.S.W., L.I.C.S.W., are available online. To access this document, visit the Hazelden Bookstore Web site at www. hazelden.org/bookstore. In the search box, insert "But He'll Change," which should bring up the product page for this book. You will be able to download a PDF of the interviews from this page.

PREFACE

Growing up, my mother told me, "It is never okay for a man to hit a woman—*never.*" Years later I was faced with that reality—I found myself in an abusive relationship.

The fear and pain I lived with forced me to leave the relationship. It was one of the hardest things I've ever had to do. Healing took time, but I finally moved on to create a new life for myself. I thought my experience with abuse was over.

Then one day, I opened the newspaper and read the results of a survey about high school students and sex. The majority of the students in the survey believed that if a man forces his wife to have sex, it isn't rape. Almost half the teens said that if a guy buys a girl dinner, she has to provide sex, and if a girl agrees to have sex and then changes her mind and the guy forces her, it isn't rape. *Someone needs to talk sense into these kids!* I thought. I could do that, but would teenagers listen to a grandmother?

I contacted a school social worker. He suggested I volunteer through the local women's shelter. I went cold inside. Could I get that close to the pain of abuse again without drudging up my own dark memories? It had been well over a decade since I broke free. I toed the dirt for a while, mulling over the idea, then made the call.

I'm glad I did. I discovered that I could use my experience to benefit other women. My long-term relationship with an abuser and the process of healing had taught me much about intimate partner violence. The training I received at the service agency connected to the local women's shelter gave me a solid foundation in the dynamics of domestic abuse. I drew on all these sources of knowledge to develop an interactive program on teen dating violence and healthy relationships. Over the course of seven years, I spoke to over seven thousand students in high school and middle school health classrooms. The students accepted me. They asked challenging questions. They wrote comments on my evaluations that said, "I didn't realize what I was doing to my girlfriend. I'm going to stop it." "Now I know why my mother won't leave her boyfriend." "I was going to get back with my boyfriend, but after hearing you, I changed my mind."

I also spoke to adults through community clubs and at the local college, teaching students in the medical field how to screen patients for domestic abuse and what to do next.

About this same time, my work life changed. I left my career to write the "great American novel" I'd always planned. As I worked on it, thoughts of domestic abuse victims continually interrupted my character development and plots—even my sleep. In particular, I kept thinking about the statements that victims use to respond to the internal voice that is screaming, "This is not right. Get out!" I began jotting down these statements in a spiral notebook. Before long, I had two full pages of statements starting with "Yes, but I love him" and "Yes, but he can be really wonderful," and ending with "If I could just love him enough, he'll change." I thought, *Someone should write a book that pushes women to think beyond these ideas. . . . Why not me?* I know the thinking and self-talk that women in abusive relationships internalize from their abusers—statements that allow women to tolerate the abuse, and resist the urge to leave. And I also know how to counter those thoughts. I know why such thinking is false and how it works to keep women trapped in unhealthy, dangerous situations. Most important, I know what healthy relationships look like and I want to give other women the words to counter their negative thinking, until they can recover their own voices of strength.

As I started to put *But He'll Change* together, I lamented to one of my mentoring therapists, "No one will publish my book. I don't have a degree in therapy." He assured me a publisher would recognize that I had the most important kind of education—personal experience. He was right. I knew what it took to heal after domestic violence.

I have written the book that I needed while recovering—one that

~ talks straight

~ tells the truth

~ explains how healthy thinking sounds

~ gives permission to care for and stand up for yourself

~ is flexible, allowing you to work on issues as they surface

It's been nine years since I jotted "Yes, but I love him" on the first line of my notebook. May the pages of this book help you identify and change your harmful self-talk, regain your self-trust, shed labels, transcend the past, and walk into a better life—a life filled with peace and joy.

A Note from the Author

This book will focus on abuse that occurs between a man and a woman, with the man being the abuser, since this was my experience. However, I invite anyone experiencing domestic abuse to use this book and to substitute the proper pronouns where needed. The components of abuse are alike in any relationship.

ACKNOWLEDGMENTS

I am grateful to those who supported and encouraged me as I worked on this project: my husband and family; the therapists, pastors, and staff of my local women's shelter, who answered endless questions; Leigh and Maureen, who read and reread the manuscript; Cathy, my gifted editor; and Sid, along with Hazelden's staff, who gave me an opportunity to speak. Thank you.

,

INTRODUCTION

Perhaps you're holding this book in your hand because your therapist suggested it. Or maybe you were wandering around the bookstore and the title caught your attention. Perhaps it's because someone bought the book and thrust it into your hands, telling you, "You must read this book." (As annoying as they may sometimes be, our friends mean well.) Regardless of why you picked it up, this book can help if you

~ repeatedly find yourself in difficult relationships

~ are struggling to stay away from a partner who causes you pain

~ realize that your current relationship isn't working out and you've had enough

~ want to model healthy self-care for your children

~ want to change what leads you into poor relationships, or are at least willing to look at other options

~ have a friend who's living in the darkness of abuse

It's difficult to admit you're currently in or once were in an abusive relationship. It is humiliating and embarrassing. I know—I lived in one for nearly twenty years. I remember how agonizing life can be. I'm here to tell you that there is another way to live, a way that doesn't include walking on eggshells, stifling your feelings, and holding back your words for fear that your partner will get angry.

If there is any question in your mind whether your partner is abusive, turn to Profile of an Abuser on pages 199–202. If you check even a few items on the list, you are on a dangerous road. The shortest test to determine if your relationship is healthy is to ask yourself, "Am I afraid to tell him how I really feel?" Can you talk openly to your partner without being afraid that he will ridicule you, discount your opinion or feelings, or lash out at you? A partner in a healthy, mature relationship will respect your opinion even if it differs from his. Healthy relationships do not include fear.

If you have already left an abusive relationship, this book will teach you the dynamics of abuse, how abusers etch self-debasing thinking on victims' spirits, and help you examine your false beliefs. It will hold your hand during the long, dark days when the urge to return to the relationship claws at your psyche. It will teach you how healthy thinking sounds and point out warning signs to help you avoid falling prey to another abusive partner. *But He'll Change* will reinforce what you know to be true: you deserve love and respect.

If you are currently in an abusive relationship, you may have given up hope that your partner will change. You may have resigned yourself to the situation as it is. Even if you feel stuck and completely powerless, I want you to know that change is possible and that you do have power. It may seem inconceivable, but changing your thinking gives you the power to change yourself. You can make a difference in your own life, even if you choose to stay with your partner. This book will help you get started.

> **NOTE:** If you are in immediate danger, call the police. If you are living in an increasingly violent relationship, don't wait any longer. Call your local women's shelter or the National Domestic Violence Hotline at 800-799-SAFE (7233) for guidance or just to talk with a compassionate person.

DOMESTIC ABUSE 101

What Is Domestic Abuse?

The term *domestic abuse,* also called intimate partner violence (IPV), is the systematic suffocation of another person's spirit. It's about power and control—one person holds all the power and uses it to control the other person, the victim. Domestic abuse includes physical, emotional, spiritual, and sexual abuse.

When we think of domestic abuse, the first thing we usually visualize is hitting, punching, kicking—physical attacks. But abuse also includes having someone do the following:

~ Call you names
~ Berate you
~ Consistently ignore your feelings
~ Throw things at you
~ Humiliate you in front of others
~ Insist on making decisions for you
~ Prevent you from practicing your faith
~ Set rigid rules
~ Judge you harshly
~ Force you to have sex
~ Make demeaning comments about your gender
~ Withhold affection (See What Is Abuse? on pages 195–197 for more examples of abuse.)

While there are several behaviors that are present in almost all abusive relationships, there are as many variations on the style and severity of abuse as there are perpetrators. Some people think abuse is about anger run amuck. Yet anger is only one of the tools used by an abuser to establish fear in the victim, making her compliant. Abuse is a choice. Anyone who can choose to hit can choose not to hit. Anyone who can choose to berate another can choose to speak kindly.

Other people think a mental health disorder or problems with alcohol or other drug use causes abuse. Although mental health disorders may be a factor in some cases, most research shows a low rate of mental health disorders in even the most violent abusers.[1] When it comes to alcohol and drugs, they only serve to make it easier for the abuser to act on his impulses.[2]

Physical violence is easy to identify as abuse because it leaves bruises on the body. We see the black eyes, the broken bones, the stitches, the blood. But emotional, spiritual, and sexual abuse are every bit as destructive—and all types of abuse leave emotional scars on your spirit. A broken arm or leg can heal in six to eight weeks. Wounds on the spirit can last a lifetime and affect every future relationship you have. It often takes a therapist to help heal them.

Who Is a Victim?

Domestic violence is a general term that refers to any abuse that occurs within a familial-type relationship; victims include romantic partners, children, or elderly people. In romantic relationships, the partners may be married, living together, or dating. Both heterosexual and homosexual relationships can become abusive, and abusers can be either male or female.

Women from the early teen years through later life can be victims of domestic abuse. About one in three high school girls dates a boy who slaps, punches, kicks, or strangles her. Females who are twenty to twenty-four years old are at the greatest risk for nonfatal intimate partner violence.[3] Thirty-seven percent of women in the United States live in emotionally abusive relationships.[4] The number of females murdered by their intimate partner has remained at about 30 percent of all female murders between 1976 and 2005.[5] Between 1976 and 2005, 5 percent of all murders by intimate partners were girls (ages twelve to seventeen) killed by their boyfriends. The group of women ages thirty-five to thirty-nine had the highest percentage of murder victims by intimates, 43 percent. Women sixty years old or more (a group less likely to report domestic violence) made up 21 percent of all murder victims by intimates.[6]

What Do Healthy Relationships Look Like?

Many women in abusive relationships have never known what it's like to be treated a different way by a man. Let's explore how healthy relationships differ from those that have turned abusive.

The beginnings of most relationships are the same. They're like striking a match: they catch fire, bursting into flame. It's called the *honeymoon period* or *limerence*. It's electric. You have butterflies in your stomach just thinking about your sweetheart. His voice is the first one you want to hear in the morning and the last in the evening. If you're a teen, you hold hands in the halls and sneak kisses behind the teacher's back. You doodle his last name with your first name all over your papers and books. I admit, some of us adult women have doodled our sweetheart's name with ours too. During this period, you want to spend all your time alone with him, getting to know each other, often neglecting your family and friends. Limerence is exciting and wonderful.

After the initial flare-up, like the match, the relationship settles into a nice, even flame. This is love. It's when you don't need to be together twenty-four hours a day to feel loved and cherished. You've built a relationship on trust, respect, and communication. If your sweetheart, God forbid, is sent on an extended business trip or a semester in France, you know you won't shrivel up, die, and blow away in the wind. You rest in the trust you've established.

From there the relationship continues to grow. You learn to negotiate solutions to problems. One person doesn't always have to acquiesce to the other's needs and wants. A healthy relationship gives you time

~ on your own
~ with your partner
~ with your friends
~ with your partner and friends

Your partner becomes your greatest cheerleader. He encourages you to find your passion in life. He wants you to develop and use your gifts and skills to become fully you. He will support your dreams as you support his. Growth and change will not threaten the relationship but keep it fresh and alive. In his book *Loving Each Other,* Leo Buscaglia says, "The very measure of a good relationship is in how much it encourages optimal intellectual, emotional and spiritual growth."[7]

Let's go back to the match image. Sometimes when you strike a match, it flares up and then goes out right away. This happens in relationships too. You experience this fabulous time of limerence. Then, one day, you look at one another and say, "What did we ever see in each other?" You break up and move on. The worst-case scenario is when you think your sweetheart is the greatest, but suddenly he announces, "It's over." Whether or not you initiated the breakup, when a love relationship ends, you go through a grieving period. In short-term relationships, the pain usually lasts 3 to 4 weeks. For women it's about 2 or 3 gallons of ice cream, a big spoon, and 16 sappy chick flicks to cry through. For men, who often work out their pain with physical activity, it can be 200 games of racquetball, 150 games of basketball, or 250 of football. For long-term relationships, the pain after a breakup can last longer. I suggest those experiencing overwhelming grief seek some counseling to help the healing process. The point is, after a period of grieving, the hurt eases and you are ready to move on.

The Cycle of Abuse

Abusive relationships start with the limerence, or honeymoon, period just as healthy relationships do, but instead of growing and moving forward, they veer off into a cycle that becomes repetitive. After spending so much time alone with your new partner, you begin to open your life to the relationships you've neglected while in the limerence stage. You're ready to spend some time with your friends or family without your partner. This causes great panic for the controlling man. He moves to *isolate* you.

This may be the first time you realize that something isn't right. You're noticing a *red flag*—that little voice inside you that says, "Something is wrong here."

In abusive relationships, there are many red flags. One of the first to appear is often *jealousy*. What makes jealousy dangerous is that it can masquerade as love. When you are dating a guy and he says he's going out with friends without you, you may feel somewhat jealous or left out. These are normal feelings. Jealousy steps over the line when your partner forbids you from going out with your friends or won't let you talk to persons of the opposite sex, especially if they were previous partners. You will hear comments such as, "Please don't audition for the musical. If you get a part, you will be at rehearsals all the time and we won't have any time together." "Don't go back to college. Between your job and studying you won't have any time for me." "Don't you love me? Don't you want to be with me?" "If you love me, you won't (insert activity or interest here)." All these appeals for your time may seem very romantic, but he is using your love to control you.

Receiving an unexpected call during the day from your sweetheart just to say he loves you sets your hearts aflutter—but how about twenty-three calls in one day, or in one hour? What about near-constant texting, asking what you're doing and who you are with? Such behaviors are other red flags that you are entering into dangerous territory. Cell phones have opened the door to *stalking and maintaining control over a victim.* The line between healthy and unhealthy becomes blurred. Yes, you love him, yes, you want to hear from him, but suddenly you feel suffocated by his constant barrage of calls questioning your every move, every moment of every day. Those love calls or text messages become threatening and a way to control you.

All of these actions illustrate one of an abuser's core beliefs—that he's entitled to be the center of your world, and the only thing in your world. However, he has no intention of making you the center of his. He doesn't want you to find a career or cause that becomes your passion. He expects that caring for him will be your only passion in life. Socializing with others is out, because you might develop a support base that will counteract his work to control you. He may move you a great distance from your family to sever your support base so he has more control of you. Some abusers even feel threatened by their own children. Murder by an intimate partner is one of the leading causes of death for pregnant women.[8]

At this point, the relationship has moved from limerence into the tension segment. He becomes more controlling and frightening—*demeaning* you, *attacking your self-esteem, playing mind games* with you. If you try to call him on his behavior, he *denies, minimizes,* and *blames* you for the problems. During the tension period, the abuser may make grand and loving gestures designed to keep you off balance so you remember who he can be. It gives you hope and keeps you in the relationship. Underneath, he's seething that he "had" to do kind things for you. In his mind, you owe him. The tension escalates until, in an effort to maintain and hold control, he erupts. This is the incident where he may berate you, threaten you, brandish a weapon to terrorize you, or beat you. Any one of these actions is not acceptable, and you are in no way responsible for his behavior. As Lundy Bancroft points out in *Why Does He Do That?* "Abuse is a problem that lies entirely within the abuser."[9]

Often the abuser has made the decision to batter even before the victim enters the picture or does anything. I could tell by the sound of my partner's footsteps coming toward the door whether or not he was going to be violent that evening; if he was, there was nothing I could do or say to stop him. He would find something—dust on the top of the refrigerator, the wrong meal for dinner, how I looked—to justify his abuse.

After the abusive incident, your partner may become contrite and beg your forgiveness. He cries and brings you flowers or expensive gifts. He promises he'll never do it again. He reminds you that if you had answered your cell phone quicker when he called or hadn't talked to that old boyfriend, none of this would have happened. He seems so distraught and grief-stricken that your focus may switch from your pain to his—exactly what he wants. You may believe him, feel sorry for him, and take him back. Suddenly, you're in the honeymoon period again, where everything is wonderful and you're sure it won't happen again—but it does.

Although it's called the cycle of abuse, it's actually a spiral. The time between incidents grows shorter and shorter. The honeymoon and tension periods shrink. The incidents become more and more violent. The result of domestic abuse is often death. On average, more than three women in the United States die each day at the hands of the men who profess to love them.[10] It's time to say, "Stop. No more."

Maya Angelou said, "When someone shows you who they are, believe them the first time." Not just the first time he hits you, but the first time he *puts you down* or *makes you feel less than who you are.* The first time he *runs over your boundaries,* or *discounts your feelings.* All of these are red flags warning you that you are in danger. (For more information, see the Cycle of Abuse on page 203.)

Destructive Thinking and Self-Talk

Abuse escalates so slowly that you may not realize where it's taking you. It starts with a derogatory comment here and a tight grip on your arm there. If you confront him, he tells you it's no big deal. He didn't mean it. You're too sensitive. As the abuse grows, he manipulates you to believe he's the one in pain and he needs you. No one else understands him. These are emotional hooks to make you feel sorry for him. You believe him and are sure that if you can just love him enough, he will change. Because you care about him, you adjust your thinking to allow you to stay in this impossible situation. Research shows that long-term exposure to emotional abuse causes chemical changes in the brain.[11] As a result, the victim's view of the severity of the abuse becomes skewed.

If you are thinking the way I did, you are clinging to the fantasy that one day he will wake up sorry for all he has put you through, that he will transform into a prince. He will recognize that you made him who he now is and will be eternally grateful to you for saving him. We are kidding ourselves. As long as he refuses to admit what he is doing, and will not get help to stop this behavior, the abuse will continue and its severity will escalate.

The truth is—if he hits you once, he will hit you again. If he humiliates you once, he will do it again. People do what works for them. If controlling you through bullying or physical attacks gets him what he wants, why would he change?

Should I Stay? Should I Leave?

Of course, I want to tell you to run away from this guy. (Actually, I would like to tell you to have him thrown in jail if he has assaulted you and to prosecute him to the fullest extent of the law.) Having been there, I know it's more complicated than that. Yet to outside observers, the choice to stay in a relationship that has turned abusive seems absurd. *Why would anyone put up with that?* they wonder.

They don't understand that what happens to women in these relationships is the same thing that often happens to kidnapping victims. It's a survival mechanism called the Stockholm Syndrome.[12] After a period, those kidnapped begin to side with their captor.

When we put this dynamic within the context of what is supposed to be a loving relationship, you can more easily understand the myriad of shackles that hold you. You love him and have known him to be loving and caring in return. You wonder why the relationship that had been so wonderful before can't be that way again, permanently.

This person whom you love most in the world, and who at first said you were perfect, now constantly declares that you are a stupid, worthless woman. Soon, he doesn't have to tell you that anymore. He has repeated it often enough that you have a nonstop message in your head to remind you. He's battered your self-esteem into the ground. He's blamed you for everything that has gone wrong, "If you had only (insert action here), everything would have been okay." He's convinced you that no one else would want you. In addition, you may feel embarrassed and full of shame for allowing the abuse to continue. You may not have any money. He's kept you from working and/or he controls all the finances. He may have taken away your car keys, or actually locked you in the house when he went out. You are exactly where he wants you to be. You are no longer a person; you're his possession. Pile on the fear that if you try to leave, he will find you and beat or kill you. How could you not feel trapped and confused?

By the time your relationship reaches the point of deciding whether to leave or stay, you are deeply entrenched and filled with fear.

The severity of your abuse may require you to break off the relationship—or it may not. Only you can decide that. This is a difficult decision and you must examine and weigh all the variables, what's in your best interest, your children's best interest, and what help is available to you. You can call the abuse hotline in your area or the National Domestic Violence Hotline at 800-799-SAFE (7233) for information on available help or just to talk to a compassionate person.

Your partner may willingly (or grudgingly) seek professional help and make the needed changes. If your partner is willing to attend counseling, carefully consider what type of therapy would work best in your situation. Some mental health professionals believe that couples counseling is effective, but only if there is no physical abuse going on. Others hold that the best approach in situations of domestic abuse is always what they call "gender-specific domestic violence treatment." This means a male batterer attends private or group therapy with other males. A professional trained to work specifically with batterers leads the group. (See Darald Hanusa's interview online for more information. See page xiii in the front of this book for instructions on accessing the interview. Also see pages 215–216 for Web sites to help you find professional help.)

I stand with those respected professionals who say the controlling partner must enter treatment for batterers. There should be no couples counseling until he has completed the program. I think you will understand why if you ask yourself whether you will feel comfortable speaking openly in front of your partner about his abusive behavior. Couples counseling can give your partner more information about your vulnerabilities that he can use to manipulate you. In addition, if he is unhappy with what you tell the therapist, you could be in danger. If he completes batterer's treatment and you decide to do couples counseling, make sure you choose a therapist trained in domestic abuse counseling.

If your partner also has a substance use problem, most therapists suggest he also complete a qualified treatment program before you consider joint counseling.

I have to be honest and say that even with treatment your partner may not change. Abusive behavior is a choice. You aren't responsible for his choice. You don't deserve any kind of abuse under any circumstance or for any reason—and you can't make him change.

If you request that he get help and he refuses, or plays games, pretending he's attending counseling but isn't, and you stay, or keep returning to him, he will feel justified in continuing the violence. You may have to get help and leave for the benefit of your children and your future. Yes, breaking up hurts. Yes, you are afraid. Please know that the pain of breaking up hurts only for a short time, then you can move on. Abusive relationships hurt 24-7-365. There were days when the pain was so bad, it took all my energy just to keep breathing.

Change can be a scary thing. It takes a lot of work. It can be painful and tough. Let me tell you that it's no more difficult than what you are, or were, doing each day to maintain the relationship.

Change is liberating! When I left my relationship, I felt, "It's too late, and I'm too old. No one will want me." I joined a group with others healing from broken relationships. Our ages ranged from twenty-six to sixty-five. Every woman who wanted to be in a loving relationship believed she was "too old" and it was "too late." The sixty-five-year-old was the first to meet someone special. Others of us followed. Read "No One Else Will Ever Love Me" and "It's Too Late to Start Over" in chapter 8. An old proverb tells us it's never too late to turn around when you are headed down the wrong path.

If you are staying because you are afraid that if you go into a shelter you will have to leave behind a beloved pet, that's not necessarily so. More and more humane organizations have foster homes for large or small animals, loving people who will care for your pet until you are in a stable situation.

Whether you choose to leave the relationship or not, you have the power to move toward healing and to recover. Even if your partner won't enter therapy, you can. (See the Jennifer Parker and Eve Lipchik interviews online for advice on finding a therapist. See page xiii in the front of this book for instructions on accessing the interviews.) If your partner refuses to let you go into therapy, ask yourself, "Does my partner have my best interest at heart?"

Leaving is one of several options. The timing is up to you. For now, you can reduce your negative self-talk and stop blaming yourself for your partner's behavior. Treat yourself with the grace and honor you would extend toward your best friend. Remember this is not your fault; you don't have to and shouldn't go through this alone. Reach out for the support that surrounds you. This is his shame, not yours. Start thinking of yourself as a survivor, not a victim. Make your choices in your own, and your children's, best interest.

> **NOTE:** Leaving a violent relationship can be dangerous. If you choose to leave, *you must work with people who can help and protect you.* Contact your local women's shelter, go to www.ndvh.org, or again, you can call the National Domestic Violence Hotline at 800-799-SAFE (7233), to learn about safe ways to leave. See Safety Planning on pages 207–211 for suggested ways to stay safe in the meantime.

If You Have Children . . .

I know as a parent, you are concerned about the safety of your children. Abuse focused on one person has a way of spilling over to other members of a family. Just hearing or witnessing violence changes a child. Statistics show that child abuse often follows spousal abuse. If your partner attacks your children, call 911. (In addition, see Ann Brickson's interview online for information on ways to help your children. See page xiii for instructions on accessing the interview.)

If you are afraid he will harm your children, and you can safely leave, do so and go to your local shelter or other safe place. If you need help leaving, contact the National Coalition against Domestic Violence at www.ncadv.org for information on resources available to you and your children through your local domestic abuse service agency. The National Domestic Violence Hotline personnel can also help you with this. See pages 215–216 for a list of some of the national hotlines and Web sites.

YOUR ROAD TO HEALING

Where Do I Start?

To create a life of peace and joy, we must face the facts and acknowledge the truth of our situations. For me, it meant admitting that I was in an abusive relationship, identifying the network of lies my partner had created, and understanding the components of domestic abuse. I had to stop blaming myself for my partner's behavior and hold him responsible. I had to face the fact that there are people in this world who will use cruel tactics to manipulate someone who loves them to get what they want. I had to learn to trust my instincts again. As a parent, I had to learn to model better self-care and relationship skills. Over time, I transcended the past and cast off the labels of "victim" and "survivor." Now I am a woman who spent a small percentage of her life in an abusive relationship. This part of my past doesn't influence my future.

> **A NOTE ABOUT LABELS:** Recognizing yourself as a victim is an important first step in recovering from domestic abuse. Then you move on to understanding you are a survivor, a person who has the power to survive in a horrid situation. These labels serve a purpose in the beginning of our healing journey, but we don't want to embrace the labels or let them define who we are. As we begin to heal, we will eventually see the abuse as one period in our lives, something that happened to us, but it is not who we are. So with time and work, labels fall away. Otherwise we spend the rest of our lives seeing ourselves as damaged. We are not damaged. We are strong and capable.

How do you begin seeing the truth of your own situation? Reading and working through this book is a good first step. It will help you recognize the negative thinking and self-talk that is keeping you stuck. If you want your situation to change, you have to take action. If this was your first experience with an abusive partner, and the relationship was short-term, this book can open your eyes to the abuser's intention and manipulating behavior. *But He'll Change* and your circle of family and friends could be enough to help you avoid future relationships with dangerous partners. However, if abusive partners have been your steady diet or you have invested years of your life in a relationship with an abuser, I recommend therapy. Abusive relationships can leave you disheartened and devastated that the relationship did not work out as you had hoped. It helps to have a therapist explore these feelings with you.

This book *should not* take the place of a therapist. It should support, not replace, the work you do in therapy. Use it as an additional tool to reinforce what you learn in your sessions and to help you between visits—during those weak moments when the old life, where you knew the score, is tugging at you. Old habits make deep grooves in our lives. Filling in those grooves and making new ones takes time and effort.

Therapy—Group and Individual

If you decide to see a therapist, be sure he or she is trained in treating victims of domestic violence. The women's shelter in your area or your doctor can refer you to a group or individual that is a trained professional. If money is a problem, ask for a referral to someone who charges on a sliding scale, such as those at a social service organization. There may also be free peer-based support groups through the domestic abuse service agency. A facilitator, not a therapist, would lead this group. For more information on how to find the right therapist, see the online interviews with domestic abuse experts (see page xiii in the front of this book for instructions on accessing this document). I hope you will be open to trying whatever is available and affordable. Have the courage to walk away from any treatment that is not working. Don't be discouraged if it takes some time to find the right place to receive the help you need. You are worth the time and effort.

I found group therapy enormously helpful in my recovery. Hearing others' stories helped me to understand my own. The other group members brought up questions I didn't know to ask. Since we were all in different stages of healing, it helped to see how those who were beyond my stage navigated through the pain. I learned two important lessons in group therapy: to extend to myself the grace and tenderness that I felt toward the other women, and that I could trust my gut feelings.

I also spent time in individual therapy to address my specific issues. It was critical to my healing.

If you won't see a therapist because you are afraid that you will have to give up your partner, let me say again, you won't. A good therapist won't tell you what to do but rather will work with you in the framework of your choices without passing judgment on you.

A therapist's job is to flip on lights along your path so you can better see and understand the dynamics and patterns of your relationship. When you come to a fork in the road, a therapist shines a light in each direction to clarify what may lie ahead. He or she will help you examine your choices and options, and talk about how to deal with them. Then you decide what direction to take. He or she will help you explore the "bungee cords" that keep yanking you back into an unhappy relationship. If you decide to leave, your therapist will give you the tools to sever those cords so you can move on with your life. Only you can choose your life path. It is work, but the work is worth it . . . I know; I've done it.

I hope that the first therapist you see will be the right one for you, but just like any working relationship, you may have to try a few until you find the one that clicks with you.

There are some red flags about therapists. If you aren't feeling some relief within a few weeks, try a different therapist. Be cautious of those who are quick to offer medications. Often the same results can occur through talk therapy. If your therapist recommends having intimate contact or a sexual relationship with him or her to learn to trust again—run. Feeling attracted to your therapist isn't unusual, but a therapist with ethics will never participate in or suggest physical contact or a sexual encounter. Report any inappropriate behavior to your state medical society or licensing board.

The Work Ahead, and Healing, Takes Work

In a world of instant gratification, it may be overwhelming to look at long-term work. I remember wanting someone to take care of me. I didn't want to be responsible for providing a roof over the heads of my children and me. I wanted to ride on someone else's coattail. He would be the knight in shining armor, caring, providing for the family, and fighting my battles. I wanted a life of ease. That's not what life is about. Life—your life, just like my life—is long-term work. What your life becomes is totally up to you. You can put off the tough stuff, or you can plunge through it and onto the right track—the one that leads to healthy relationships.

Giving up what you have is frightening. You love him. When you picture yourself without him, you see a horrifying scene. Think about the special toy or blanket you had as a child, the one you carried everywhere. Remember how you couldn't sleep without it tucked under your arm? When it was lost, you felt the whole world was crumbling around you. Remember how anxious or hysterical you were and that horrid pain in your stomach from fear that your precious toy was gone forever? You cried until it was found. Where is that toy today? Chances are, it was discarded years ago or tucked away in a keepsake box. You grew out of it. You no longer need it because you've matured beyond that stage of your life. The same thing will happen with this painful relationship. You'll lay it aside and move on to a new and higher level of self-confidence.

It will take hard work to rebuild your life. You know what hard work is. Look at the effort you have put into your relationship. You are a victim, but you are also a survivor. You know what it takes to make it through each day. A therapist or your local women's shelter will help you develop a support and security system and guide you through the legal system, if necessary.

HOW TO USE THIS BOOK

There is no right way or wrong way to use *But He'll Change.* Use it in whatever way it works for you.

I do suggest that you begin by looking over the chapter subheadings. If something clicks with you, you'll know where to begin. If you're feeling weak and are afraid you will cave in and return to an unhealthy relationship or be taken in again by your former partner, or a new abusive partner, look for the chapter subheading that matches most closely what you're telling yourself. Reading it will and remind you why pursuing that relationship isn't in your best interest. Remind yourself that you deserve better. Also, consider what you are modeling to your children or the children around you.

I suggest you read the text aloud to engage your hearing. Read it to yourself in the mirror, over and over. Look deep into your eyes and tell yourself you deserve a happy life.

Relationships are complex and individualized. In my responses to the statements, I've included every circumstance I could think of. Some of the paragraphs will not fit your situation. A bold highlighter can make the information that does speak to you stand out.

At the end of each statement section is a list of "Truths," or affirmations. I suggest you read them aloud as often as needed, until you move the lessons from your brain to deep inside you, replacing the false beliefs. You may develop your own personal affirmations as well. During my healing, I wrote mine on the back of old business cards and carried them in my pocket. I took them out often and read them. In weak moments, just putting my hand on the small rubber-banded, well-worn packet gave me strength.

The affirmations are followed by "Issues to Explore." These are suggested topics to talk about with your therapist or contemplate on your own.

Consider having a notebook or journal handy to

~ write answers to the exercises in the text and jot down any issues raised

~ add any additional statements, personal to your situation, and your responses

~ list questions or concerns you want to explore on your own or with your therapist

~ note the important points that you discover during therapy or group work

Journals are a safe place to express your feelings and clarify your thoughts. Later, you can measure your healing process by reviewing your journal. If you are still living with your controlling partner, keep your journal and this book well hidden or at a friend's house.

At the end of this book, in the appendix, you will find information to help you better understand the many facets of abuse. Also included is a list of books and Web sites that I found helpful, and those suggested by therapists and friends. Transcending the past means healing all aspects of your life. It's a lifetime process to become who you are meant to be; these books and sites can help.

In addition, excerpts from interviews I conducted with domestic abuse experts can be found in a PDF document online. These therapists discuss important issues, such as forgiveness, how living with abuse affects children, and how abusers can change. For instructions on how to access this document see page xiii in the front of this book.

You are the only one who can change your life. Change begins with the first step. A little prayer for help can get you on your way too.

FINAL COMMENTS TO VICTIMS OF ABUSE

While you likely have said to yourself, "If only I'd done things differently," "I was such an idiot," or "Look what I've done to my children," remember to be kind to yourself. I asked those I interviewed, "How do victims forgive themselves?" They all responded by saying: forgiving yourself means you've done something wrong. Abuse victims didn't do anything wrong. They have nothing to forgive. Loving, trusting, and expecting the best from the person you love is the right thing to do. The one who betrays that trust is the one who has done wrong.

Let me add one last thing. If you and your partner are separated but still engaging in sex—stop it immediately. If you are separated but are still talking with him about anything other than the children's welfare—stop it immediately. As long as you stay connected to this person, you are expelling your important energy into an empty hole. Put the energy into healing yourself. At least you have a willing participant.

IF YOU ARE A FRIEND OR RELATIVE
OF A VICTIM OF ABUSE

I don't have to tell you how painful it is to watch someone you love struggle in an abusive relationship. I know it breaks your heart and you feel helpless. On average, it takes seven attempts to leave before the victim can finally sever the cords and stay out of the relationship. It's discouraging to watch someone you love return to an abuser. Do your best not to criticize her for going back. She has to do this in her own time. Let her know that though you may not understand what she is doing, you will respect her decisions and continue to care about her.

When I started volunteering with a domestic abuse agency, I thought shelter volunteers swooped in on their white horses, picked up the victim, and carried her away to a better life. I soon learned that abuse is about power and control. Victims need to take back the power over their lives. If you take control of the situation, you become the one who is holding the victim's power.

So how can you help? First and foremost: *If you witness violence, immediately call the police.*

This is a painful and overwhelming process. You may not have the energy to walk with your friend through this darkness. That's okay because you can be the one who plants the first seed. Tell her you see what is happening to her and she doesn't deserve it. Tell her there is a way out when she is ready. Then provide her with the hotline number for the shelter in your area or the national hotline.

If you are willing to become more involved, there are some additional things you can do.

~ If she confides in you that her partner is abusive, tell her you believe her. Stay calm. If you start demonizing him, she will cling tighter to him. If you get angry and start ranting, you will be carrying her feelings. Let her experience her own anger. Just confirm what she says, and let her know that you are concerned.

~ Tell your friend that the violence is not her fault. In violent relationships, the abuser always blames the victim for everything that goes wrong. Remind her that she is not responsible for his behavior.

~ Tell her she deserves better. Don't tell her she's crazy for staying with him. That only confirms to her what she's been hearing all along—she's stupid. She won't believe she deserves better.

~ Remind her of all the wonderful things about her. She's only heard that she is worthless. She needs to remember her good traits.

~ Document her injuries. Take pictures of her bruises. Write the date on the back of the photos. Keep a calendar with notes of when you saw injuries and where they were located on her and what they looked like. You can keep the calendar even if she hasn't admitted what is happening. Your notes are admissible in a court of law to show that the abuse has been ongoing and is not just a one-time incident. One-time incidents are often dismissed.

Your documentation could be crucial to prove domestic violence.

~ Look over the safety planning information on pages 207–211. Tell her how you can help her. For example, keep a suitcase of her clothing, emergency documents, and funds, should she have to leave quickly. Have a signal that she needs help, a shade pulled, a plant placed in a window, a code word. Have her tell you where she is going and when she will return so if she doesn't show up when expected, you can notify the police.

~ Contact the shelter in your area for information regarding support services for your friend. Tell your friend that when she is ready to leave, you know where she can get help. Provide her with the shelter's phone number. If she is ready to talk to them, have her call from your house.

Caution: *Never put yourself in danger by confronting the batterer.*

Helping someone in this difficult situation can be draining for you. If you need support, your local shelter or a therapist (experienced in treating domestic violence) can support and direct you as you emotionally support your friend.

But He'll Change can help her if she is ready to read it. However, if she is still living with her partner, she can't take it home with her. You may have to keep it at your house.

On behalf of victims everywhere, I want to thank you for not ignoring what you see. You are a gift to those in pain and an important part of ending violence against women.

MY STORY

I met my partner in a bookstore. The moment our eyes met, it felt as if a bolt of lightning shot through me (just like in romantic fiction). He introduced himself and kissed my hand. For a young woman who had been a nobody in high school to have this attractive, intense guy focus on me was heady and wonderful. I was hooked.

Most people think that only those raised in violent homes go on to abusive relationships. That isn't true. I didn't come from a home where my parents beat up each other. Sure, Mom and Dad had arguments, but more often, Dad would chase Mom around the dining room table for a kiss—the two of them laughing like teenagers. My sisters and I would roll our eyes.

My parents raised me to have a kind heart. Along the way, wanting to be a "nice person," I evolved into a people pleaser. Everyone else's needs and wants came before my own, even to my detriment.

When I met the bookstore guy, a guy who believed the only way he could keep a partner was by holding all the power and control in the relationship, our sicknesses melded perfectly. I gladly turned over control of my life to him because it made him happy. He gladly accepted it. We became a couple. His passion and desire for justice captivated me. I saw his anger focused on others. I never thought it would come around and land on me.

The first time he hit me was less than a year after we were married. He slapped me. I was stunned. Over the next few days, I convinced myself that it was a fluke and it wouldn't happen again. It did. During the fourth incident, he hit me so hard on the side of my head that he popped my eardrum.

This was back in the 1970s, when people didn't talk about this kind of thing. Ashamed, I didn't want to tell anyone, but my ears were ringing and I had trouble hearing. After three days, I knew I had to get medical help. I didn't tell the doctor that my husband hit me. I said I got hit in the head with a ball but asked him to check both ears.

Today, medical personnel screen patients for abuse by asking, "Do you feel safe at home?" In the 1970s, medical personnel didn't get involved. The doctor simply told me to stuff cotton in my ear and keep it dry. It would heal in about three weeks. No questions asked.

After that incident, my mother's words came back to me: It is never okay for a man to hit a woman—*never.* On a calm evening, I sat beside my partner and said, "Look, I love you with all my heart. But if you continue to hit me, I will have to leave." He stood up and went into the bedroom, shutting the door. I could hear him crying. This was way out of character for him. He believed men don't cry. My people-pleasing heart said, "What have you done? You're a horrible person."

When he came out of the bedroom, he said, "I never thought you'd hurt me like this."

I remained silent, my heart aching.

He said, "I thought you loved me."

"I do love you."

"You said you would leave me."

"Yes. If you hit me, I will have to leave."

"Then you don't love me."

My people-pleasing heart was screaming, "Tell him you love him. Tell him you'll never leave—no matter what." My gut shouted, "Shut up. Don't retract the statement." I didn't take back the ultimatum. I set a boundary that day. I didn't know I set it until much later.

After that evening, he did abstain from hitting me; the physical violence in our relationship was limited to him shoving, grabbing, and pinning me up against the wall with his arm across my throat. He ratcheted up the emotional abuse. At that time I didn't recognize the red flags. I believed abuse only involved hitting and punching; now I know that abuse can also be verbal and psychological.

He used *constant criticism* and *name-calling,* telling me that I was a stupid, worthless woman who couldn't do anything right, repeatedly. Over time, the Stockholm Syndrome took over. My partner didn't have to tell me I was stupid or worthless. He had brainwashed me to the point where the message was constantly in my head to remind me.

Through *humiliation* and *ridicule* my partner taught me that to express my own feelings and needs was selfish. He made it clear that it was not safe for me to disagree with him.

If I said I wanted or needed something, he'd *withhold* it. He was generous with other things, but not with what I wanted most—he deliberately *withheld his love and acceptance.*

Ignoring my feelings was common. When a drunk at a party made advances to me, my partner ignored my gestures for help. A friend noticed my signals; he leaned toward my partner and said, "Your wife needs your help." My partner said, "I know, but I'm not going to help her." He was sending me a clear message that he held the power and control in our relationship and he would decide whether he would be there for me. My thoughts were: *If he won't be there for me with a drunk at a party, how can I be sure he'll be there for me if my life's at stake? Will he help me or will he let me twist in the wind?* I couldn't be sure.

Another red flag behavior in our relationships is called *messing with your mind,* or *crazy making.* If you've seen the classic 1944 movie *Gaslight* with Ingrid Bergman and Charles Boyer, you know exactly what messing with your mind is. Boyer would move Bergman's things around or hide them so Bergman thought she had misplaced them. He dimmed the gaslights and implied to her that she was imagining things. Systematically, he attempted to make her and those around her believe she was going crazy. His goal: put her in an asylum and control her wealth.

Though my partner's motives were different (I didn't have any wealth), he told me I had said and done things I hadn't. He'd change his rules without telling me and expect me to know what he wanted. What was okay one day was not necessarily okay the next. He played many different mind games with me to destroy my self-trust and self-esteem.

Through ignoring my feelings and messing with my mind, he taught me that I couldn't trust him. In addition, I couldn't trust myself—I was going crazy. I felt helpless and trapped.

Those who know my story often ask why I stayed. First, I stayed because I truly loved him. Then, because I had sympathy for him; I knew he had pain in his life, and I wanted to save him. Also, we had children and I thought I was a stupid, worthless woman who couldn't do anything right. How was I going to take care of my children on my own? Besides, he told me if I tried to leave, he'd take the children from me and I'd never see them again. I was brainwashed to the point where I believed he could. Then I stayed because he had a .357 Magnum—a big gun. He never threatened me with it, but I knew it was there, loaded in his desk drawer.

Let's go back to that boundary I set so many years before. Toward the end of our relationship, my partner slammed me against the wall and put his arm across my throat, pressing in until spots swam in my tear-filled eyes. He said, "You gonna leave me now?" I had thought he refrained from hitting me because I hadn't made him angry enough. I believed it was only a matter of time until he'd step over that line. After all, he'd swaggered over my boundaries in all areas of my life. Pinned against the wall that day, I realized he hadn't hit me because he didn't want me to leave him. So if I said I'm leaving, what would keep him from beating me or pulling out that gun? I didn't know. I stayed because he had bound me with ropes of fear and I felt suffocated.

I can't begin to find words to explain how painful it was to live with this man. I used to wake up in the morning before the alarm clock rang. I'd lie there and pray, "Dear God, please don't let it be morning. Please give me just one more hour before I have to face my life today." Then I would roll over and look at the clock. Some days God granted that hour, others God didn't.

There are as many different "final straws" as there are victims. For me it was when he began to turn the violence on our children. Often women can do what seems the impossible when their children are at risk. He'd hacked off my love for him with each violent, disrespectful act toward me—and then the children.

It came to a head at a Fourth of July party. Our children were away visiting my parents, so it was just the two of us. We were staying with Robert and Jane in our old neighborhood. All our old friends from the block were there. I was sitting in the living room listening to one of Robert's great stories. My partner came to the kitchen door. He said, "Come out and sit with me while I play cards."

I said, "Okay. As soon as Robert is finished with his story, I'll be out."

"No. You'll come now."

As I turned to Robert to excuse myself, my partner charged across the room and grabbed me by my arms. He pulled me up into his face and began screaming at me. The stunned neighbors watched in silence as he berated me. They knew nothing about his violent temper. He was the first one to help dig a neighbor's garden, shovel a driveway, or work on a car. He shoved me toward the bedroom and told me to pack—we were leaving. I did what he said. One of my friends followed me to the bedroom and asked, "What is he doing? Is he really like this?" Shame burned my face.

My partner had been drinking all day. I was afraid to get in our vehicle with him. I asked my friend to have Jane speak to him, believing that if anyone could calm him down, she could.

While packing, I could hear Jane talking with him in the kitchen. He was yelling; she kept her voice calm. When I went to the kitchen door, they were nose to nose. He was screaming in her face. I was afraid he would hit her. He snatched the suitcase from me and walked out to the car. I didn't move. He returned and said, "Let's go." Everything around me went black. I saw myself standing in a dark room. The door was open. There was light out there, but it didn't shine into the blackness. A voice said, "If you don't leave now, the door will close and you will live in this darkness forever." I looked at my partner. For the first time in our life together, I told him no.

"I'm not going with you," I said.

His eyes narrowed. The purple-blue veins in his neck stood out, crimson spider-webbed across his face. He started batting around the chairs and hitting the table, bellowing threats. The other men at the party gathered around him and walked him to the vehicle. I followed, pulled the suitcase from the back, opened it, drew out my clothing, and then quickly returned to the house. He left.

He called me from the gas station a block away. "Are you coming with me?" he demanded to know.

"No."

"If you don't come with me now, you can never come back."

"Okay," I said and hung up. I knew our relationship was over. I had committed the worst offense against him anyone could—I defied him. The reality of my leaving demolished the wall of protection. There was no longer a reason to restrain himself from harming me.

I waited up all night. I figured it was two hours to where we lived—ten minutes for him to get the gun—two hours back to kill me. I believed I'd be dead in less than five hours.

He didn't come back. The next day, I flew to my parents' home and contacted a lawyer. It was over. I was divorced within ninety days of filing. A couple months later, I realized I'd left him on Independence Day. God has a sense of humor.

When I left the relationship the mantra running through my head was, *Why couldn't he love me? What's so awful about me that he couldn't love me?* It took therapy to turn around that thinking and teach me that it wasn't me—it was him.

I was desperate to be well—to be able to trust myself again—to get my thinking right so I would never find myself in that position again. I had to stretch muscles I never knew I had. It was difficult and uncomfortable. Fierce determination drove me to pick myself up and move forward. I sought help from pastors, therapists (who charged on a sliding scale), and support groups. I examined, then clipped, the strings that held me in the relationship and kept putting one foot in front of the other. I took every challenge my therapist threw at me and filled my journal, writing my way through the anger I had stuffed for so long. When that didn't give me relief, I pounded on my bathtub with a towel, freeing the rage. (A wet towel makes a beautiful sound on porcelain.)

Over time, I climbed from the deep pit, stepping on boulders of, "I don't deserve this," "There is light at the end of the tunnel," "I must do it for my children's sake," and "I can do this." I filled small cards with Bible verses and affirmations, such as: "You are in control" and "God did not give us a spirit of timidity, but a spirit of power and love."[13] and carried them in my pocket. Touching them gave me strength. I read everything I could get my hands on and struggled to replace the negative thoughts that kept me stuck in the past with the truth of what I deserved and could have.

In weak moments when I was afraid I'd have to go back to him, I called a girlfriend who would come, sit and listen, then assure me there was no good reason to return to the abuser. There were times when I took a step or two backwards and faltered. I tried not to chastise myself for those moments, but continued to urge myself on. There was a goal in sight. I learned to take back my power without wielding it as a weapon or using it as a shield to protect me from pain, to express my needs, and to look at men not as the enemy, but as equals. I learned to be wise about protecting my children and me. I tasted the sweetness of a peaceful life and wanted more, so I trudged through the agony of facing my abuser in court. As my self-respect grew, my abuser's power over me diminished.

Those aching muscles started to hurt less over time. My self-esteem began to grow. I rediscovered myself and found that I could provide for my children and myself. We made sacrifices and went without a lot. It wasn't easy. With the guidance of therapists, my children and I stumbled along, reconstructing our lives. We came out stronger and wiser. Our reward was living in a peaceful home that held no fear—one that allowed us to focus on our own lives instead of keeping one disgruntled member happy.

I never thought I could be happy living without a partner. I was. Ironically, then I met a man. I fell in love—not madly with unabandoned passion as in my youth—but with quiet dignity. Hopeful, but terrified, I allowed the bud of love to open at its own pace. I revealed to my partner who I was and learned that I did not have to change for him to love me. Five years later, we were married. My husband is my knight in shining armor, but he doesn't fight my battles for me; he knows that I am capable of dealing with problems on my own. He supports me, listens to me, and encourages me.

My prayer is that this book will help you rewrite your self-talk so that you remember the special and unique person you are. As Rabbi Harold S. Kushner says in his book *How Good Do We Have to Be?*, "One of the basic needs of every human being is the need to be loved, to have our wishes and feelings taken seriously, to be validated as people who matter."

May it be so for you.

Chapter 1

SEEING HIM AS

ALL-POWERFUL

AND THE CENTER

OF MY WORLD

Love is one of our basic needs.

Both women and men have visions of what love is and what being loved looks like. Because we are all individuals, our interpretations vary somewhat.

A woman's vision may look something like this: She and her sweetheart will forge a partnership where the two are helpmates, create a home, share household responsibilities, encourage each other in their professions, plan for a family, and raise children. In the evening, they will curl together on the sofa and relax while they share their day, basking in each other's love and devotion. Yes, there may be arguments, but they will only serve to clear the air and be followed by great makeup sex. This is a healthy, reasonable vision and one that is often similar to what men envision.

When a woman receives attention from a seemingly intelligent, insightful, giving, and romantic gentleman, she may come to believe he is her perfect mate. However, if this man is controlling and abusive, the aforementioned behavior is a sham.

She thinks that he's asking questions about her because he finds her fascinating. However, whether deliberate or just a facet of his entitlement nature, he is actually collecting data (her vulnerabilities, fears, and hopes) that he can use later to control her. While she is thrilled that he listens to her point of view, he is actually learning how she thinks so he can bend her will to his. While she is excited that he thinks she's so wonderful and sexy he can't keep his hands off her, he's pressing her to become sexually involved to hook her emotionally.

She thinks she has fallen in love with someone who shares her vision. She hasn't. His plan is to draw her into his vision, a world where he is the center of the universe. He expects that she will recognize his intelligence and superiority and forsake all others (including herself, her dreams, and passions in life) to serve him.

A controlling man has a sense of entitlement. To him, a woman is inferior, put on this earth to meet his every need—be it a clean and well-cared-for home, cooking his favorite foods, or sex the way he wants it and when he wants it. Her needs and wants never enter his vision. To him they don't exist.

When he believes she has fallen for him, he begins to play mind games with her, whittling away at her self-esteem, using the information he's acquired from her to keep her locked in the relationship. He deliberately creates chaos in her life to keep her confused and focused, not on what he is doing—setting up the privileged position for himself—but on how she can make the relationship better. Seeking to make sense of his erratic manner, she often tries to overlook his behavior and reinterpret it, accepting responsibility for the problems. He, on the other hand, believes he is taking his rightful position as master of his domain.

He may be a well-respected member of the community. Often people will remark how lucky she is to have such a great guy. But inside their relationship, the life they share is so different from the one he originally professed to want that she can't make sense of it. His constant accusations that it is all her fault causes her to question herself: *If everyone thinks he's wonderful, it must be my fault.*

For some abusers, children are either unwelcome—he makes sure there are none—or they can become tools to tie his partner to him. He may keep her barefoot and pregnant or hurt the children to get back at her.[14]

Over time, it's likely that he's brainwashed her to believe that he has the power to fool legal and psychological experts, so she better not attempt to leave him. He may have taken control of the money so she has none and convinced her she is so incompetent she could never care for the children on her own. If she tries to run away, he's confident that the courts would take his word over hers. He'll get custody of the children, and she'll never see them again. He assures her that no one can protect her from him. Wherever she tries to hide, he will find her, drag her back, and make her pay for the trouble he claims she has caused.

Over time, she comes to accept that he holds the power. Like a kidnapping victim, she falls prey to Stockholm Syndrome and begins to side with her "captor," internalizing his negative opinions of her.

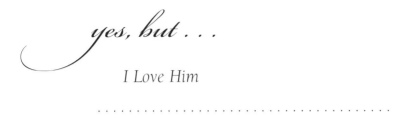

I Love Him

· ·

In my journal during a quiet moment, I will examine the following questions:

~ *What do I really love about my partner?*

~ *What would I change about him?*

~ *Do I really love him or do I love an image of how I think he could be, or how he has been for short snippets of time?*

People do what works for them. My partner is abusive toward me because it serves him well; it gets him what he wants. He seeks to gain complete power and control over our relationship. The only time he meets my needs is when he thinks he may lose me. At that point, he'll say and do whatever it takes to keep me in the relationship. Yet as soon as he feels secure, he returns to his old behavior. This is the cycle of abuse. (See page 203 for more information on the cycle of abuse.)

As time goes on, the good times—the honeymoon period (where he is Mr. Wonderful)—will shrink and incidents of abuse (verbal or physical battering) will quickly follow the tension period (where Mr. Wonderful becomes irritated, short-tempered, and dissatisfied). In abusive relationships, the severity of violence usually escalates over time. The result is often emotional or even physical death. Staying in this relationship could also jeopardize the lives of my children.

As wonderful as the honeymoon period is, I now recognize that the abuse will always follow. His past behavior predicts his future behavior. As long as I participate in this cycle, it will continue. If my partner refuses to work with me to stop this cycle, I must decide if I'm willing to continue this relationship and endure the likely consequences.

I want to feel loved and valued. My partner uses this need to manipulate me so that he holds all the power and control of our relationship. He dangles a carrot—the promise of what our relationship could be—before me, but never lets me reach it. I struggle to win his affection so that he will make me feel loved and valued. I must learn to love and value myself.

Showering him with love will not stop the abuse. I can't love him into changing. My being a doormat or martyr won't make him love me or treat me any better. He must choose to change. He tells me repeatedly that he wants to change. He hasn't. Since his past behavior predicts his future behavior, I know his promises are empty. If he truly wanted to change, he would do what it takes and get professional help.

Instead of telling myself things that keep me stuck, my self-talk will now build me up. Over time, I'll become stronger. I won't let my love for him tie me to him. When the time is right, I will leave. For now, I will continue to work toward healing.

Sometimes we must close our hearts to those who hurt us.

I'll learn to show myself honor, love, and respect. I must love myself before I can love anyone else. Despite what my partner says, taking care of myself is not selfish. Loving and respecting myself is not conceited.

I am worthy of love.

TRUTHS

- Sometimes we must close our hearts to people who hurt us.
- I love and value myself.
- Although I love him, that doesn't mean I have to stay with him.
- As wonderful as the honeymoon period is, abuse will follow.
- His past behavior predicts his future behavior.
- Without his cooperation, the only way to break the cycle is to leave.
- Taking care of myself is not selfish.
- Loving and respecting myself is not conceited.
- I am worth loving and worth treating right.

ISSUES TO EXPLORE

1. Why I feel I must make him love me
2. Why I fear taking control of my own life
3. How I can change my role in the cycle of abuse
4. How it would feel to be in a loving relationship
5. What a loving relationship would look like

yes, but . . .

I Miss Him (or I Need Him) and
Can't Live without Him

. . . .

I've focused all of my energy on him and our relationship. I'm not sure who I am by myself anymore. I've turned my power over to him partly because I was afraid I couldn't make it on my own; I didn't believe in myself. Also, I thought it would prove my love for him. Lacking in self-esteem, I tried to find fulfillment through his successes rather than working toward my potential and individual dreams. This isn't healthy.

It's time that I change my thinking and work on my self-esteem. I am a whole person. I may need to develop some sides of my character that have been lost or repressed. I am capable of this work.

Why do I think I can't live without him? What would I really miss about him? A partial list includes the following:

~ *Saying that I have a partner in life*

~ *A warm body next to me*

~ *Sex*

~ *Talking to someone*

~ *My dream relationship*

~ *His repairing things around the house*

In my journal, I will list other things I would miss.

What are some things I will not miss about my partner? Examples include being

~ *berated*

~ *lied to*

~ *forced to live by his rules*

~ *ignored or neglected when I need him*

~ *called stupid, worthless, ugly, lazy, and incompetent*

~ *battered*

~ *forced to serve his needs and wants*

~ *in constant fear of what he will do next*

~ *forced to make up excuses to other people for his bad behavior*

~ *humiliated in public*

In my journal, I will list other things I will not miss.

If I walked away now, I would miss the dream I had for this relationship, not the man. There is a good chance that I can one day have that dream relationship with someone else. First, I must heal myself.

When I am ready, I must let go of the past so I can move on with the future.

TRUTHS

- If I left, I would miss the dream I had for this relationship, not the man.
- My dream will never come true with this partner.
- If I let go of the past, I can move on to the future.
- After healing, I can build a happy relationship with someone else.

ISSUES TO EXPLORE

1. Facing the truth of this relationship
2. Developing a realistic dream
3. Rebuilding my self-esteem
4. Rebuilding my ability to trust my feelings and intuition
5. Envisioning what my life without him would feel like

He Is Everything to Me

My partner is my whole world. Allowing him to remain the center of my world isolates me and puts an end to my dreams and goals. This will stop me from achieving my purpose in life—which is not to keep him happy. There is a greater one for me to discover. I'll work to recover the dreams and goals that I had to release and begin to focus on achieving them. I'll fight through the fear of failure. It will take work, but I can do it. I know what hard work is. I've put plenty of hard work into this relationship.

In a healthy relationship, partners encourage each other to explore their gifts and talents to the fullest. They are each other's biggest advocate.

TRUTHS

- I am a whole person. I don't need anyone else to complete me.
- I'll work to uncover the dreams and goals that I released and begin to focus on achieving them.
- In a healthy relationship, partners encourage each other to explore their gifts and talents.
- Someone who loves me will be my biggest advocate.

ISSUES TO EXPLORE

1. Fear of failure
2. How he became the center of my world and how to ease him out of that position
3. Rediscovering my dreams and goals

Suggested reading:

When Love Goes Wrong: What to Do When You Can't Do Anything Right by Ann Jones and Susan Schechter, Harper Perennial, New York, 1993

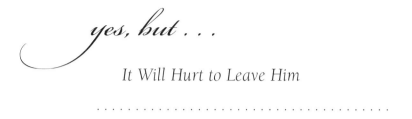

yes, but . . .

It Will Hurt to Leave Him

. . . .

Yes, it would be painful to leave, but how painful is it to be with him if he continues his current behavior? In my journal, I will answer the following questions:

~ *On a scale of 1–10, with 10 being the most painful, where does my relationship fall?*

~ *Will I feel some relief to be free of this partner?*

~ *Am I more afraid that he will hurt me if I leave or that I will regret leaving him?*

I will carefully evaluate my situation and should I decide to leave, I will seek help from my therapist or the local women's shelter, or I will call the National Domestic Violence Hotline at 800-799-SAFE (7233) for information on how to leave safely.

The hurt from leaving would be temporary. It will go away. If I stay in an abusive relationship, I'll suffer nearly every moment of my life.

He is not the only person I'll ever love. If I leave the relationship, rebuilding my life will be my top priority. This will take some time, but eventually I may choose to turn my attention to meeting someone new. I will have an opportunity to build a relationship that includes the following:

~ *Trust*

~ *Respect*

~ *Understanding*

~ *Patience*

~ *Communication*

~ *Humor*

~ *Companionship*

~ *Mutuality*

~ *Honesty*

TRUTHS

- Ending a painful relationship is not easy, but it is possible.
- Breaking up hurts for a short period.
- This is not the only person I'll ever love.

ISSUES TO EXPLORE

1. Safety planning with a therapist or women's shelter professional (see Safety Planning on pages 207–211)
2. Grieving this relationship
3. Taking care of myself
4. Dealing with my anger and fear

yes, but . . .

I Have to Do What He Wants
or He Won't Love Me

. . . .

To keep me from noticing that he has positioned himself as the center of my world, he creates confusion in my life. His game is to make me feel that I am lacking and must be better if he is to love me. However, no matter how loving and giving I am, he points out that it is not good enough. I now realize that he will continue to raise that bar so that I'm never able to win his approval. His power comes from denying me the goal I seek—to be in a mutual loving and nurturing relationship.

Someone who loves me would not threaten me or force me to do something I don't want to do or be someone I'm not. Love doesn't mean I must become a puppet or that I must meet his perceived need at the expense of my own.

Asking me to do what feels uncomfortable or putting me in a risky place shows his lack of love and respect. This includes sexual situations and the way he wants me to dress, drive, act, and so on.

If I have to change before he will love me, it's control not love. Someone who loves me will respect who I am and allow me to be myself even if he doesn't always agree with me. While it's important to be flexible and it's okay to acquiesce at times, I don't need to give up my comfort zone, beliefs, and feelings to make someone else happy.

Not everyone will agree with me or like me. That doesn't mean that I'm unlikable or a horrible person. It means that we have different ideas, opinions, and interests. Conflict can be healthy and lead to positive change as long as it is nonabusive.

TRUTHS

- Someone who loves me will respect who I am and what I think even if he doesn't agree with me.
- I don't need to give up my beliefs and feelings to make someone else happy.
- Not everyone needs to like me.
- I have a right to be who I am.
- Conflict can be healthy and lead to positive change as long as it is nonabusive.

ISSUES TO EXPLORE

1. My need to have everyone like me
2. My need to earn my partner's love
3. What activities and behaviors are outside my comfort zone and are nonnegotiable for me

Suggested reading:

Do I Have to Give Up Me to Be Loved by You? by Jordan Paul and Margaret Paul, Hazelden, Center City, MN, 2002

yes, but . . .

I Have to Do What He Wants
Sexually or He Won't Love Me
(or He'll Find Someone Else)

. . . .

Great sex happens between two people who come freely and willingly to the encounter and are as concerned about their partner's pleasure as they are about their own. This means that each partner would not ask, expect, or force the other partner to engage in any activity against his or her will. (For more information on sexual abuse, see What Is Abuse? on page 197.)

Forcing a partner to engage in sexual activity is rape even if you are married.

People in healthy relationships build satisfying, pleasurable, and intimate sexual lives based on trust and respect.

Threatening to go outside the relationship for sexual satisfaction is how he intimidates and attempts to coerce me into doing things that are not in my pleasure range. This shows his selfishness and lack of concern for my feelings. Someone who loves me would never expect me to participate in sexual activities that hurt, embarrass, or threaten my life.

TRUTHS

- Great sex happens between two people who are as concerned about their partner's pleasure as they are about their own.
- Satisfying, pleasurable, and intimate sexual lives are based on trust and respect.
- I do not participate in a sexual activity that hurts me, embarrasses me, or threatens my life.

ISSUES TO EXPLORE

1. What I am looking for in a sexual relationship
2. Building blocks for intimacy

yes, but . . .

I Have to Tell Him Everywhere I Go and What I Do So He Can Reach Me

or

He Shows Up Unexpectedly Because He Loves Me

. . . .

Early in a relationship, these behaviors may seem flattering and look like love and concern. They are not. These are power and control issues. I will maintain control of my life.

Trust is a foundational part of a relationship. Requiring me to report in, and to be available so he can check up on me, shows his lack of trust—and so do his unexpected appearances. These actions are disrespectful. People who love each other, trust each other. Though my partner may say he does this out of love, it's control, not love. Following me is a form of stalking.

If his former partner was disloyal, he should have dealt with that issue before he entered into a committed relationship with me. He can't deal with past hurts if he's too busy being paranoid about me. If he wants to get over it, he'll get professional help and work on healing. If he doesn't want to deal with it and expects me to live in his paranoia, he needs to know that I won't.

Often, the person doing the accusing is the one who is being untrustworthy. If my partner accuses me of being unfaithful, there's a good chance that he is being unfaithful himself. Cheaters often throw guilt and blame on their partners as a way of justifying and camouflaging their own bad behavior.

If my ex-partner follows me or tries to contact me after I've told him to stop, I will contact the police and report his stalking and unwanted contact. I can obtain a court order to tell my ex-partner to stay away from me. I will also keep a record in a date book or on a calendar of any stalking or unwanted contact from him, including dates, locations, damage to property, and physical attacks. I will save (in a safe place) any unwelcome mail, e-mail, and voice-mail messages I receive from him. These are documents I can use in court to prove his violent intentions and inappropriate behavior.

TRUTHS

- Trust is the foundation of a healthy relationship.
- People who love each other trust each other.
- Often, the person doing the accusing is the one who is being untrustworthy.

ISSUES TO EXPLORE

1. Learning to trust my instincts
2. Looking at my history of trusting others
3. Components of real trust in relationships
4. Appropriate circumstances to keep a partner abreast of my activities
5. Finding a safe place to keep documents, pictures, and other material that show his violent behavior
6. When to go to the police and when to go to court for an order of protection

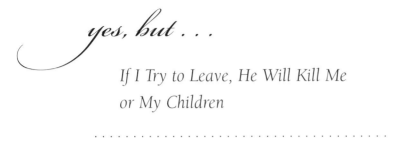

If I Try to Leave, He Will Kill Me
or My Children

. . . .

I take my partner's threats seriously.

The current situation has no chance of improving. If I stay, it will only grow worse and more violent. I could easily end up dead. He could also kill my children. I will document my injuries and any injuries to my children and keep this record in a safe place. Such documents may prove that my children and I need protection from him.

Leaving is dangerous. I will carefully weigh the safety issues for my children and me, then make my decision in our best interest. Should I leave, I'll take advantage of all available help. I'll seek help from my therapist and/or call the abuse hotline in my city or the National Domestic Violence Hotline at 800-799-SAFE (7233) for help creating a safety plan. I'll work with the police, show them my documentation, and obtain an order of protection or restraining order. I will tell my friends and family the truth of my situation so that they can be on guard. I'll notify my place of work, my neighbors, and my children's teachers and school personnel.

Part of my partner's power comes from keeping the abuse a secret. Speaking the truth ends that hold on me. I will tell others what is happening.

People who care for me will lend a hand. They will watch for my former partner should he come near me after I have an order of protection. They'll be an extra pair of hands, helping me transition into a new and better life.

I will raise my children in a home filled with love and peace.

TRUTHS

- I'll surround myself with supportive people.
- I can work with the court system to protect my children and myself.
- I will tell the truth—no more secrets or pretending.

ISSUES TO EXPLORE

1. How to protect myself
2. How to protect my children
3. How to create a safety plan and a plan to leave the relationship
4. What to expect and not expect from the court system

Suggested reading:

Breaking the Cycle of Abuse: How to Move Beyond Your Past to Create an Abuse-Free Future by Beverly Engel, John Wiley & Sons, Hoboken, NJ, 2005

Getting Free: You Can End Abuse and Take Back Your Life by Ginny NiCarthy, Seal Press, Berkeley, CA, 2004

yes, but . . .

If I Divorce Him He Will Take My
Children from Me or Will Have the
Children Alone for Visitation

. . . .

Just because my partner says something does not make it possible or true.

He says he will take the children away. There is no proof that he can do that. If he shows a history of abuse through police reports and medical records, the judge is unlikely to give him custody of the children. If the children are teens, the judge will most likely consider their feelings. The court can appoint an attorney to protect my children's interest. I will ask my lawyer to suggest an attorney who knows about the effects of witnessing abuse on children. A court-appointed therapist, trained in domestic violence issues, can evaluate my children and advise the judge that my children are safer with me.

He says his friends will testify against me. Lying on the witness stand is perjury. His friends won't risk going to jail for him. He's bluffing to force me to stay.

Yes, it is possible that he could get visitation, but if my attorney has had experience in domestic violence litigation, he or she can work with the court-appointed psychiatrist to show that my partner is abusive. The judge may order supervised or limited visitations. If any harm comes to the children, I will report it to the police immediately.

TRUTHS

- Just because my partner says something does not make it possible or true.
- I can work with the court system to protect my children and myself.

ISSUES TO EXPLORE

1. How to find an attorney who litigates domestic violence cases
2. Finding support people for my children within the court system

He Is a Good Provider

While I may like the trappings that my partner's income gives me, I'm paying a huge price in my spirit if I trade my safety, peace, and happiness for this lifestyle. As much as I may fear losing the income my partner provides, I know that safety must come first. I can begin to gain new skills that will help me find a new or better job and build my own financial security.

I'd like my children to continue their varied activities, but what they are learning from my relationship is dangerous for their future. Their safety and well-being is at stake. A loving, safe home is more important than all the activities and things money can provide.

TRUTHS

- I will not trade my safety, peace, and happiness for a lifestyle.
- I can build a financially secure future for myself.
- A loving, safe home is more important than all the activities and things money can provide.

ISSUES TO EXPLORE

1. Creating a plan to learn a new or higher-level profession
2. Identifying needs and limiting wants

Chapter 2

DENYING AND

MINIMIZING HIS

BEHAVIOR

Amid her partner-created chaos, to suppress the pain of the abuse, a woman may become numb to what is happening. She may accept her partner's claims that she is blowing things out of proportion and is too sensitive. *Things aren't really so bad,* she tells herself as she continues to hope for the best.

Feeling confused and powerless, she grasps on to the slightest appearance of change in her partner to convince herself that things are getting better. She stops trusting her gut feeling that things are not right. Struggling to make sense of the situation, she rewrites what she sees to match her hopes for the future.

Her partner may have maneuvered her into a parent-child relationship. She, as the child, submits to his demands and trusts what he tells her over her own feelings. If she becomes upset, he, as the parent, acts nonchalant and tells her she is overreacting and melodramatic—minimizing his behavior. If she makes a mistake, he berates her and punishes her. He blames her for anything that goes wrong. Over time, she stops standing up for herself and loses the ability to see his actions for what they are, a way to assure he holds the power and control in the relationship. She may think she can hold on to the good side of her partner and will away the bad side. In truth, she cannot divide his personality. If she stays, she will live with the good *and* bad.

yes, but . . .

He's Not All Bad

or

*He Has a Really Sweet and
Wonderful Side*

. . . .

Although I'd like to believe that the bad side of him will go away and only the good side will remain, his past behavior has shown that it's not likely to happen. As long as I stay or return to the relationship, he thinks it's okay to continue his abusive behavior. It is not okay.

His actions indicate that he neither respects nor loves me. His occasional show of affection and elaborate gifts are a hook to keep me tied to him. When he senses I am pulling away, he draws me back with words of love and false promises. These moments of indulgences don't change the fact that he continues to hurt me. His actions speak the truth. (See the Chart of Coercion on pages 205–206 for more information.)

I will not accept abuse. If the whole person includes abusive qualities, I'll prepare to end the relationship. Without professional help, his past behavior will continue to determine his future behavior.

All people have good and bad qualities. My partner's bad qualities affect my safety and self-esteem. That is not okay or acceptable. These qualities won't go away unless he wants to change, seeks professional help, and makes a genuine effort. People do what works for them. As long as I remain with him, he has no reason to change.

Should he go into therapy after I've left him, I will not return to him until he has taken responsibility for his actions and shown a commitment to treatment by regular attendance for the length of time his therapist suggests. I have the right to end the relationship at any time.

TRUTHS

- Actions speak the truth.
- I have the right to end the relationship at any time.
- Change requires hard work and looking within myself.

ISSUES TO EXPLORE

1. Seeing and acknowledging the total person
2. If he seeks treatment: what information I would like from his therapist to help me determine if he is fully cooperating

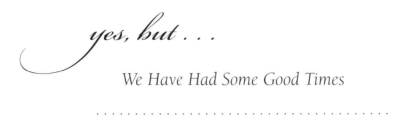

yes, but . . .

We Have Had Some Good Times

. . . .

The good times are a temporary oasis among the horrible times and are used to placate me into thinking he had changed. Even though he occasionally does something wonderful and romantic, he often ends up wrecking the moment and blames it on me.

As much as I'd like the bad times to go away, they won't. He believes our problems are my fault. He can't or won't try to understand my needs. He belittles me and calls me selfish. He refuses to attend counseling to deal with his controlling and abusive behavior. Without his cooperation, nothing can change.

Couples counseling is not an option until he enters therapy and completes the work on his own issues.

If I stay and he doesn't deal with his behavior, the bad times will continue to escalate, as illustrated in the Cycle of Abuse (see page 203). I don't deserve abuse. I deserve a relationship that has more good than difficult times and no abuse.

TRUTHS

- I will not minimize, justify, or deny what happened.
- I deserve to be in a relationship that is not abusive and that has more good times than bad.

ISSUES TO EXPLORE

1. The difference between assertiveness and aggression
2. The good times in our relationship, the things he has done to wreck those times, and the bad times

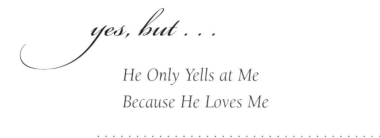

yes, but . . .

He Only Yells at Me
Because He Loves Me

. . . .

He says if he didn't care about me, he wouldn't bother to yell. Even though I tell him it hurts my feelings, he continues. He claims I'm "too sensitive." This is his way of justifying his bad behavior. Contrary to what he says, he isn't trying to make me a better person. By calling me names and saying hurtful things, he's systematically trying to undermine my confidence and self-worth. He hopes that I won't feel worthy of anyone better than him. It's his way to keep me. I won't buy into this. (For more information on emotional abuse, see What Is Abuse? on pages 195–196.)

His behavior toward me has nothing to do with my worth or value. It has to do with who he is.

I am worthy of love and respect.

As Stephen Covey says in *The Seven Habits of Highly Effective People,* each of us has an Emotional Bank Account. According to Covey, "An Emotional Bank Account is a metaphor that describes the amount of trust that's been built up in a relationship. It's the feeling of safeness you have with another human being."[15]

Someone who loves me will fill my account with understanding, kindness and courtesies, kept promises, clarified expectations, honesty, loyalty, trust, and unconditional love, as I will do for him. When my account is filled, minor infractions will not drain it.

Dishonesty and abuse (physical, verbal, emotional, spiritual, or sexual) are major infractions that drain an Emotional Bank Account. These behaviors have no place in a healthy relationship.

TRUTHS

- His behavior is not about trying to make me a better person.
- I am worthy of love and respect.
- Someone who loves me will fill my Emotional Bank Account.

ISSUES TO EXPLORE

1. How to fill my own Emotional Bank Account
2. Healthy ways to discuss differences

Suggested reading:

The Verbally Abusive Relationship: How to Recognize It and How to Respond by Patricia Evans, Adams Media, Cincinnati, OH, 2003

yes, but . . .

My Children Need Their Father

· ·

My children deserve a father who
~ *loves and cherishes them*
~ *recognizes their uniqueness*
~ *acknowledges their needs and seeks to fill them*
~ *joins with me in shaping and molding them into healthy and happy adults*

My partner demands my full attention. He manipulates any situation so that he—and not my children—remains the focal point of my life. His behavior shows a lack of empathy for the children and me. To focus on my partner at the expense of my children's needs is harmful to them. They don't deserve a home filled with tension, fear, and violence.

It is emotionally abusive for children to watch their mother suffer. It tells children that it's okay to harm women and that women should tolerate such treatment. This isn't a message I want them to receive. Whether I leave or stay, I will speak about abuse to my children using age-appropriate language. (See Ann Brickson's interview online for more information. See page xiii in the front of this book for instructions on accessing the interview.)

My children deserve a loving and supportive father. He is responsible for his relationship with them. He has a choice to be a loving parent or not. I can't force him to change. If his behavior drives away his family, that is his choice.

Parents must discipline their children, teaching them right from wrong, without the use of violence or threats of abuse.

It's better to raise my children in a single-parent home filled with love and support than to allow their father to abuse them. *If I see any sign that he is physically abusing the children, I will immediately go to the authorities. If I see any signs that he is emotionally abusing the children, I'll remove them from the situation.*

My children deserve to live in a peaceful home. They should witness a healthy, happy, and loving adult relationship. That's how they learn to be loving and caring partners.

How I live my life influences how my children live theirs. I can show them how to make good life and relationship choices.

TRUTHS

- My children deserve
  - to be raised in a loving and supportive home
  - to be nurtured and encouraged to find and develop their gifts
  - a loving and supportive mother
  - a loving and supportive father
  - to witness a healthy, happy relationship between their parents
  - to live in a safe home

- Every member of a family should feel important, respected, loved, and cared for.
- It's better to raise my children in a single-parent home filled with love and support than to allow their father to abuse them directly or indirectly.
- How I live my life teaches my children how to live theirs.
- When disciplining, parents should not use violence or threaten abuse.

ISSUES TO EXPLORE

1. How to talk to my children about abuse
2. How to build my children's self-esteem
3. Learning and modeling assertiveness
4. Learning nonabusive discipline and parenting skills
5. Parameters for reporting abuse to the child welfare authorities
6. How to protect my children until we can safely leave (See Safety Planning on pages 207–211)

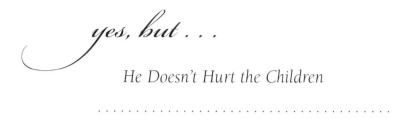

yes, but . . .

He Doesn't Hurt the Children

Children from violent homes live in fear and tension. Even if my children don't witness the abuse, they are aware it's happening. They hear the altercations. They are afraid for me. If they try to intervene, my partner could harm them. (See Ann Brickson's interview online for more information. See page xiii in the front of this book for instructions on accessing the interview.)

Children often unjustly blame themselves for the violence, thinking if they were good, Dad wouldn't get angry and hurt Mom. They feel guilty because they can't protect Mom, or because they're afraid to try.

I will tell my children that the abuse is not their fault and they cannot protect me. I will teach them what to do to protect themselves when my partner erupts.

Children who witness abuse often internalize their fear, pain, and rage, causing health problems or severe acting out against others. They may have a low frustration tolerance and often lower levels of empathy toward others. They often have issues with trust, safety, self-esteem, and boundaries. Though it may be indirect, the abuser's behavior influences and scars children. In short, he is hurting the children.

Children learn the behavior modeled for them. If they grow up in a violent and chaotic home, they may repeat the behaviors they've witnessed by becoming violent toward their partner or accepting abuse from their partner. If I must stay, I will develop a safety plan with them and learn how to support my children emotionally so they become healthy adults. If I decide to leave, I will develop a safety plan to remove my children and myself from this dangerous and unhealthy situation. This safety plan may include age-appropriate responses and action from my children. I will model how to set healthy boundaries.

TRUTHS

- Children from violent homes live in fear and tension.
- Children learn what they live.
- Watching and hearing abuse harms children.
- My children deserve to feel safe and protected.
- I will teach my children that they are not responsible for another person's bad behavior.

ISSUES TO EXPLORE

1. How to help my children deal with their emotions
2. How to help my children learn that abuse is not part of a loving relationship or family
3. The truth of how my relationship is hurting my children
4. Modeling healthy choices for my children
5. A safe location for my children to go in an emergency
6. If age appropriate, how to work with my children to determine code words that tell them to leave or call the police

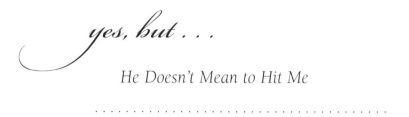

yes, but . . .

He Doesn't Mean to Hit Me

. . . .

Whether to hit or not is a choice—his choice. It is not my fault. Even if my behavior makes him feel angry, his response is his choice. If he hits me, it's because he wants to hit me; he means to. He is trying to control me through fear. What I say or do does not release him from the responsibility of choosing his reaction. He doesn't hit his boss or coworkers when he is angry at work. He doesn't hit others. He hits me. That makes it a choice.

Hitting me leaves bruises not only on my body, but also on my spirit. Broken bones and physical bruises heal. Bruises to my spirit can remain forever and affect every relationship. Therapy can help me heal these bruises.

He is minimizing, denying, and blaming me when he says:
- ~ *"It was an accident."*
- ~ *"I did not hit you that hard."*
- ~ *"You are making a big deal out of nothing."*
- ~ *"You make me so angry or frustrated I can't help myself."*
- ~ *"If you would just (fill in the blank), it would not happen."*

In my journal, I will list other ways he minimizes, denies, or blames me.

When he claims that he doesn't mean to hit me and then cries and begs me to forgive him, it's a manipulative counteraction designed to placate me with false hopes and trigger my sympathy. The same is true for the flowers and other gifts he brings. He promises to get help but either he doesn't (he cannot find a therapist or program he likes) or doesn't stick with it (quitting after only one or two sessions of therapy). His promise to change has held me in this unhealthy situation. I will not buy into it any longer. Whether or not I forgive him, I don't have to stay with him. (See Robert Enright's interview online for more information. See page xiii in the front of this book for instructions on accessing the interview.)

People do what works for them. As long as he gets what he wants by physical or emotional abuse, he will continue his abusive behavior. If I succumb to his antics, he will assume it's okay to abuse me as long as he tells me he's sorry. If I stay and he doesn't get treatment, the abuse will most likely continue to grow and become more violent. (See the Cycle of Abuse on page 203 for more information.)

TRUTHS

- Abuse is not love.
- Hitting is a choice.
- I deserve to be treated with respect.
- I have a choice to stay or leave.

ISSUES TO EXPLORE

1. Identifying and resolving the issues that hold me in this relationship
2. Danger signals/red flags to watch for in future relationships
3. Trusting my feelings and intuition

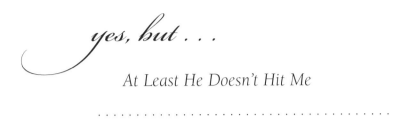

At Least He Doesn't Hit Me

"Each of us is responsible for creating an environment of warmth and consideration for those we love."

LEO BUSCAGLIA, *LOVING EACH OTHER*

Emotional abuse is as bad as physical violence. While physical abuse leaves bruises and broken bones on the body, emotional abuse leaves deep bruises on the spirit. Bruises and broken bones heal. The bruises left on the spirit can remain forever and affect future relationships. I will not justify, minimize, or deny his emotional abuse. (For more information on emotional abuse, see What is Abuse? on pages 195–196.)

He's emotionally abusing me when he
- ~ *controls me through jealousy*
- ~ *withholds love*
- ~ *ignores my feelings or doesn't take them seriously*
- ~ *calls me derogatory names*
- ~ *tells me I'm stupid, worthless, selfish, lazy, sloppy, ugly, or some other negative word*
- ~ *tells me that he's only saying these things to help me become a better person*
- ~ *tells me that he has heard others say things about me*
- ~ *humiliates me in front of others*

~ ignores me or gives me the silent treatment

~ denies my reality, beliefs, and values

In my journal, I will list other ways he emotionally abuses me.

As long as I put up with emotional abuse, he'll continue to do it. Even though I've told him that it hurts my feelings, he continues. This shows he lacks empathy for me.

Verbally abusing me in front of the children is his attempt to destroy the children's respect for me. This, too, is a control issue. He uses the children to help beat me down by encouraging them to tell me I am stupid and/or to hit, punch, or kick me. I won't remain with someone who teaches my children to disrespect me.

My partner claims that his derogatory comments are intended to help me become a better person. I am the only one responsible for improving myself. I'm an intelligent and worthwhile person, capable of determining where I need to grow and making the necessary changes. I will not tolerate my partner's emotional abuse. If needed, I can get compassionate help from a therapist to heal my bruised and broken spirit.

He may not be hitting me now, but emotional abuse is often the precursor to physical abuse.

TRUTHS

- Emotional abuse is as bad as physical abuse.
- Emotional abuse often precedes physical abuse.
- I won't justify, minimize, or deny his emotional abuse.
- A loving partner helps to create an environment of warmth and consideration.
- I can heal my bruised and broken spirit.
- I am an intelligent and worthwhile person.
- I am responsible for making myself a better person.

ISSUES TO EXPLORE

1. How emotional abuse affects my life
2. Understanding the tactics of an emotional abuser

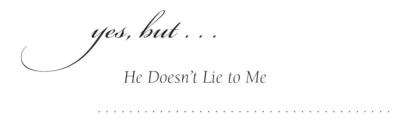

He Doesn't Lie to Me

Just because he tells me he would never lie doesn't mean he always tells the truth.

He sets me up to believe he's truthful because, under the guise of being honest, he tells me things that hurt me. Since I would never say such things to anyone, I believe that he's being painfully honest. However, his intention is to undermine my self-esteem while building up himself. These lies have a threefold purpose:

1. To convince me that he's honest at any cost—especially at the cost of my feelings

2. To convince me that I'm less than I should be

3. To show me how wonderful he is because he's "honest"

Examples of his lies include the following:

~ *He tells me he has opportunities to cheat on me but does not.*
     A man chooses whether or not to put himself in situations that give him an opportunity to be unfaithful. My partner tells me this to hurt, humiliate, and demean me. There's an underlying threat to his comment. He's really saying I'm lucky he didn't act on his feelings *this* time. If I don't do what he wants, he'll find someone else.

     Also, he tells me how great he is because he remains faithful. He expects me to be grateful because he did the right thing. In reality, the right thing should be the norm, not the exception.

~ *He tells me he has had an affair.*
     He tells me this to hurt, humiliate, and demean me. He communicates that I'm "not enough" or "not good enough," so he

goes elsewhere for sexual fulfillment. He blames me for his affair.

To have an affair is a choice. A man with principles who isn't happy with his sex life talks to his partner and together they work toward improvement. He doesn't use force or threats to make his partner do anything that hurts or makes her uncomfortable. My refusing to participate in a sex act, or not having sex often enough (in his opinion) doesn't give my partner the right to go elsewhere.

~ *He tells me that he is sorry for hitting me.*

If he were sorry about hurting me, he would stop. He doesn't hit his boss. He doesn't hit his friends. He hits me. Hitting is a choice. Anyone who can choose to hit can choose not to hit. He isn't sorry.

~ *He tells me I am stupid, worthless, and ugly.*

I'm intelligent, capable, and attractive. He is systematically destroying my self-esteem so I won't leave him.

~ *He tells me that no one else would ever love me.*

There are nice men in the world who would treat me with love and respect. I can love someone else.

In my journal, I will list his other lies and examine his purpose for using them.

TRUTHS

- He does lie to me.
- He uses honesty as a guise to demean me.
- If he were sorry for hurting me, he would stop.

ISSUES TO EXPLORE

1. How to sort out the truth from the lies
2. Determining whether or not to confront him about his lies
3. How to respectfully speak the truth to others

At Least I Don't Have It
as Bad as Others

. . . .

I don't have to qualify my pain. I wouldn't ignore my broken arm because someone else has a broken leg. In the same way, I won't ignore what is happening in my relationship because someone else is enduring abuse that is more severe. All abuse is unacceptable, be it physical, emotional, spiritual, or sexual.

Even though I may not have it as bad as others do, this relationship is costing me

~ *self-respect*
~ *self-esteem*
~ *the dreams and goals I once had*
~ *my children's respect*
~ *my safety*
~ *the safety of my children*
~ *my children's self-respect and self-esteem*

TRUTHS

- I don't have to qualify my pain.
- All abuse is unacceptable.

ISSUES TO EXPLORE

1. How to embrace the belief that I deserve a healthy, happy relationship

2. What this relationship is costing me

3. What I want in a relationship

yes, but . . .

He Must Love Me—He Gets Jealous When I Talk to or Spend Time with Other People

. . . .

Mutual trust and respect are the foundation of a healthy relationship. My partner's level of jealousy does not indicate how much he does or does not love me. Rather, it indicates that he is trying to gain power and control over me. While his jealousy may have felt flattering at the beginning of our relationship, now it is serving to isolate me from other people that I love and care about. If I stay, over time he'll likely require me to reduce the number of people in my life to only him. It's unfair and unreasonable to expect me to prove my love by ending my relationships with friends or family members and giving him my constant attention.

In a healthy relationship, socializing with others doesn't threaten either partner.

Creating a rift between my family and me (or my friends and me) is one way that he isolates me, giving him more power. Telling me that he loves me so much he wants more time with me is an attempt to flatter me into isolation. His jealousy will not determine with whom I associate.

I will decide who my friends are, based on my own experience and feelings.

I'll be wary of his claims that

~ *my friends have it in for him*

~ *my friends are envious and do not want me to be happy*

~ *my girlfriends flirt with him when I'm not around*

~ *my friends aren't really my friends because they talk about me behind my back*

~ *my family members are bad people*

People who love each other don't try to control each other. They trust each other unless one proves untrustworthy. He may accuse me of flirting with another man when I know I wasn't. Smiling and being friendly is normal, polite behavior. I won't let him mess with my mind and make me feel guilty for things I haven't done.

TRUTHS

- Mutual trust and respect are the foundation of a healthy relationship.
- Jealousy doesn't indicate how much someone loves you; healthy, mature relationships do not include jealousy.
- In a healthy relationship, spending time with friends and family isn't threatening to either partner.
- A healthy relationship leaves space for other friendships.
- People in a loving relationship don't try to control each other.

ISSUES TO EXPLORE

1. Setting up healthy boundaries
2. How I'd like to balance time with a partner and time with others
3. Holding on to my support base

yes, but . . .

He Must Love Me—He Wants to
Be with Me All the Time

. . . .

While this constant togetherness may have felt good in the beginning, it now feels stifling. In healthy relationships, partners spend time together, time together with each other's friends, and time alone with their own friends. They also have individual time.

Under the guise of love, my partner has isolated me. Isolating tactics that my partner uses include the following:

~ *Becoming jealous when I talk to other people*

~ *Getting angry when I spend time with my friends*

~ *Always wanting us to be alone*

~ *Wanting my constant undivided attention*

~ *Calling, e-mailing, or texting me several times a day*

~ *Checking up on me to see what I'm doing and where I've been*

~ *Accompanying or taking me everywhere I need to go*

~ *Following me/stalking me*

~ *Screening my mail and phone calls*

~ *Showing up unexpectedly*

These behaviors aren't acceptable. This is not a healthy way to relate. If I buy into his demands for my undivided attention, it will not only feed his desire for more control but will also cause me to lose my rights and freedoms. It serves neither one of us and will harm me.

I have the right to enjoy myself whether I'm spending time with or apart from my partner. I don't buy into the guilt or fear that he will make me pay for having a good time with my friends or participating in activities that don't include him.

TRUTHS

- A healthy relationship gives each person time to do their own thing, time apart, and time together.
- A healthy relationship is built on trust and respect.
- A healthy relationship allows each other freedom.

ISSUES TO EXPLORE

1. Trust
2. Dealing with his false accusations
3. Crazy making or messing-with-my-mind behavior

*It Doesn't Matter That I Quit Doing
Things I Enjoy or That He Made
Me Quit My Job*

. . . .

If I quit doing the things I enjoy, I allow my partner to control my life. This is a power issue. His power comes from denying me the opportunity to do the things I love and the things that would build my self-esteem.

It *does* matter when someone else tries to use power over me. I'm in charge of my life. I won't be with someone who tries to control me.

He pressures me to quit my job so that

~ *I'll become financially dependent on him and can't leave*

~ *he will be able to destroy my self-esteem more easily; there will be no positive performance reviews or comments from a boss or coworker to counter my partner's claims that I am inept*

~ *he will be the only one in my world and have my full attention*

He tries to get me fired from my job by

~ *calling me repeatedly at work*

~ *showing up and disrupting the office by disturbing my coworkers or humiliating me in front of everyone*

~ *annoying my boss by talking with him or her about my job performance and salary, how the company should be run, or what he sees as my personal flaws*

I won't allow him to badger, humiliate, or shame me. Making my life miserable is his way of preventing me from reaching my dreams.

In a healthy relationship, each partner encourages the other to grow and flourish.

TRUTHS

- It *does* matter when someone else tries to use power over me.
- I will maintain my power.
- I will do things that I enjoy, be it work or other activities or hobbies.
- I will develop my gifts and talents.

ISSUES TO EXPLORE

1. Maintaining my safety
2. Maintaining my personal integrity
3. Developing career and life goals
4. Creating financial security for myself

yes, but . . .

It Doesn't Matter What Other People Think

or

My Friends and Family Don't Understand

. . . .

A long and trusted friend is honest with me. If my friends and family members tell me that they're concerned about my partner's behavior, I need to listen. My friends have insights and a perspective that I may not see. After listening to their concerns, I will carefully evaluate what they tell me before making a decision about my relationship.

If I'm reluctant to listen to others' comments, I need to ask myself if it's because they're speaking a truth that I don't want to hear. It's time to be honest with myself. I won't live in denial any longer.

Although I'm afraid that others will think I'm stupid for allowing myself to be in this situation, I'll reach out for help. Being too embarrassed to ask for help will only prolong my situation and prevent me from moving forward. Others will see me as brave for taking action.

While it's true that my friends and family members may not understand exactly what I'm going through, that reality doesn't have to keep me stuck in this relationship. I can reveal the truth of my situation, and people who care for me will be willing to help. If my partner comes near me after I've filed an order of protection or restraining order, my friends can call the police. My friends will help me transition into a new and better life. They will respect me for having the courage to change.

TRUTHS

- I will carefully evaluate what my friends tell me.
- I will not allow my partner to turn me against my friends.
- I will not allow him to isolate me from my friends and family.
- People care about me and encourage me to take care of myself.
- I can reach out. Others will be glad to help me.

ISSUES TO EXPLORE

1. Reconnecting with friends and family
2. How to share the truth of my relationship with my friends
3. How my friends can help me

It Doesn't Matter What Names
He Calls Me

Whether or not he means what he says, it's not appropriate to call me names and humiliate me in public or private. Telling me that he's only teasing or that I'm too sensitive is his way of minimizing his behavior. He's intentionally ridiculing me.

If I allow him to continue, I'll eventually begin to internalize his negative messages about me. Repeated name-calling is a brainwashing tactic intended to disarm me and take away my power by making me feel bad about myself. His power comes in denying me what I deserve—respect.

In healthy relationships, partners express grievances in a nonabusive manner, through listening and talking. Partners don't fight dirty using name-calling, intimidation, or threats to get their way. They listen without interrupting. They don't tell their partners how they should or shouldn't feel. They respect their partners' views even if they don't agree with them.

He has the choice to fight fair or dirty. Fighting dirty shows his lack of respect for me.

If my children continually hear my partner call me names, they will think it's appropriate behavior. They'll learn to disrespect me. I won't raise my children in a home that teaches them to disrespect anyone.

TRUTHS

- It's not okay to call me names and humiliate me in public or private.
- In healthy relationships, partners aren't abusive when discussing grievances; rather, they listen and talk.

ISSUES TO EXPLORE

1. Fighting fair
2. Dealing with conflict constructively

It Doesn't Matter That He Insults
My Religion, Race, or Ethnicity

It *does* matter. He may say he's only kidding, but he's still being disrespectful. These kind of jokes aren't appropriate in any situation. Someone who loves me celebrates who I am and where I have come from.

In healthy relationships, partners honor each other, including their different backgrounds.

His insults say something about him. He's trying to put me in a "step-down position" from him. It's a tactic to isolate me from my religion or peers. I won't buy into this or tolerate it.

Making derogatory comments about my race or ethnicity in front of our children will make them feel bad or ashamed of who they are. This is not okay.

TRUTHS

- Ethnic, racial, or religious jokes aren't appropriate.
- People who truly love me will respect who I am and where I have come from.

ISSUES TO EXPLORE

1. What it means to be part of my ethnic group
2. Things about my heritage that make me proud and enrich me

It Doesn't Matter That He Flirts
with Other Women

. . . .

It *does* matter. It is disrespectful to me that he flirts with other women, telling them how hot or sexy they look, holding them closely while dancing, and creating an intimate atmosphere between them with looks, winks, and a lingering "thank you" kiss. It's not only inappropriate, but also humiliating for me when others notice his overt behavior. He knows that it hurts me, yet he keeps doing it. This tells me that he's not concerned about my feelings. Whether I'm present or not, it's not acceptable for him to flirt with other women.

In a committed and mature relationship, partners are attentive to each other and respectful of each other's feelings. (For more information on sexual abuse, see What Is Abuse? on page 197.)

TRUTHS

- In a healthy relationship, partners are attentive to each other.
- Partner's respect each other's feelings.
- It's not appropriate for partners in a committed relationship to flirt with others.

ISSUES TO EXPLORE

1. How to set clear boundaries regarding outside relationships and behaviors
2. How to talk to a partner about expectations for behavior with people of the opposite sex

yes, but . . .

It Doesn't Matter That He Withholds Affection When He's Angry

. . . .

Withholding affection, giving the silent treatment, or ignoring me is a power and control issue. It's a means to manipulate me and coerce me to do what he wants. It's not appropriate behavior in a mature relationship.

In a healthy relationship, partners may cool off for a reasonable length of time (take a time-out) and then sit down, calmly discuss the problem, and seek resolution.

TRUTHS

* Partners in a healthy relationship discuss problems and work them out.
* Even when angry, partners treat each other with respect.

ISSUES TO EXPLORE

1. Healthy ways to resolve problems in a relationship
2. How to appropriately use time-outs with a partner

yes, but . . .

*He's Learned His Lesson by My
Leaving—Now We Can Get
Back Together and Everything
Will Be Okay*

. . . .

I won't try to fool myself. If I return before he has sought professional help and completed the prescribed treatment, he'll most likely slide back into his old ways of treating me. He may behave for a while, but eventually he'll begin to abuse me again. Without getting the appropriate help, his past behavior will always predict his future behavior. (See the Cycle of Abuse on page 203 for more information.)

Because I am negotiating for my life, if he goes into treatment, I reserve the right to verify that he is seeing the therapist regularly and confirm that he is actively working his recovery program and changing his behavior. I have the right to know what behaviors I should expect and not expect. The facility where he is receiving treatment should provide me with that information. (See Darald Hanusa's interview online for more information. See page xiii in the front of this book for instructions on accessing the interview.)

    If he fulfills his treatment plan obligation, before I return I will talk with his therapist so I can evaluate his progress. If there is any indication that he is attempting to manipulate or control me or I feel that he still has the potential to be abusive in any way, I'll end the relationship. I also maintain the right to decide at any point that the relationship is over no matter what his state of recovery may be. The safest time for me to leave is while my partner is in treatment.

I am cautious of his smooth talk and promises. I've heard them before. He knows what hooks usually bind me to him. I will remain strong against his pleas. While bullying or sweet talk has always worked for him in the past, it will no longer work.

TRUTHS

- Without treatment, my partner's past behavior will predict his future behavior.
- I will be strong when he pleads for me to return to him.
- The safest time for me to leave is while my partner is in treatment.

ISSUES TO EXPLORE

1. How to avoid being drawn back into the relationship
2. How to know if he really has changed
3. How to communicate clear boundaries regarding acceptable behaviors of my partner
4. How to best use my time while he is in treatment

yes, but . . .

This Can't Be Happening—I Am Not One of "Those Women"

"You can't change what you don't acknowledge."

DR. PHIL MCGRAW

It's real and worse than I care to admit to myself. It makes no sense. I don't understand why anyone would behave this way. The truth: It *is* happening. My partner is abusing me.

As much as I would like to think that our lives are really the picture-perfect scene we present to the world, it's not true. Abuse does exist within this relationship. Though I may have had a slanted view of whom I would expect to be a victim of abuse, I now know that abuse crosses race, gender, religious, sexual orientation, and economic lines. It slid into my life and took over. I will begin the work to change my life.

I won't let shame prevent me from getting help. This is not my shame; this is my partner's shame.

By admitting what's happening, I teach my children to see the truth and to understand that bad behavior isn't okay. I also teach them that it's not their fault. They cannot control other people's behavior or reactions. We are responsible for our own behavior. To be proactive about life means you don't allow yourself to remain a victim any longer than you have to for safety's sake.

I will tell this secret.

TRUTHS

- I will acknowledge the truth about my situation.
- Abuse is not something that happens to a certain section of the population. It crosses race, religion, gender, sexual orientation, and economic lines.
- I will make healthy decisions for my children and myself.
- This isn't my shame, but my partner's.
- I won't keep this secret.

ISSUES TO EXPLORE

1. Facing the truth about violence and abuse
2. How to move forward

yes, but . . .

Sooner or Later, He'll See What
He's Doing and Stop

. . . .

Without getting professional help or attending batterer's treatment, the odds that my partner will turn into Prince Charming and stop abusing me are slim to none. He comes from a different point of view that won't change by itself. Regardless of what I do or say, he'll never see things the way I do. He'll never want the things I want for this relationship. It hurts me deeply to admit this, but I must face it so I can deal with it and decide what I want to do.

His use of abusive tactics has allowed him to have his way for a long time. He is unlikely to change. Even if he chooses to stop the physical violence, he'll most likely increase the emotional abuse. This is a coping skill, and he'll cling to it. As long as I stay with him, he'll bully me. I cannot fix him. I can only fix me.

I choose to focus on healing my pain and learning how to meet my own needs.

He only straightens up if I threaten to leave. Within a short time, he slides back into his old behavior. It's time to break the cycle of abuse.

If he truly wants to change, he'll get professional help and end the abuse. If he doesn't go into treatment, I must weigh the situation and make decisions in my children's and my own best interests. (For more information on the Cycle of Abuse, see page 203.)

I have a choice to stay with the current situation or, as scary as it seems, to step out, heal, and meet my own needs. If I remove myself from the relationship, I can focus on my own healing. Counseling would be a good choice for me.

If he goes into therapy and actively works on his issues for the duration of the batterer's program, I will evaluate where we both are and decide if I want to continue this relationship. I reserve the right to speak to his counselor and know that he has actively participated in the treatment plan and has shown a sincere desire to change. If my partner doesn't want me to talk with his therapist or tries to paint me as controlling because I checked his progress, I'll recognize that he is trying to manipulate me to keep the situation as it is. If he has changed, he won't feel threatened if I communicate with his therapist.

No matter what the state of his recovery, I reserve the right to end the relationship at any time.

I refuse to spend my whole life waiting for this relationship to transform magically. Instead, I can use my energy to heal myself and move forward with my life.

TRUTHS

- This man will never treat me with love and respect. Staying is a waste of my time.
- I can't change my partner's behavior.
- I'll focus on healing my pain and learn how to meet my own needs.
- No matter what the state of my partner's recovery, I reserve the right to end the relationship at any time.

ISSUES TO EXPLORE

1. Learning to meet my own needs
2. Grieving the lost dream
3. Questions for his therapist

Suggested reading:

"The Healing Separation: An Alternative to Divorce," in *Rebuilding: When Your Relationship Ends* by Bruce Fisher and Robert Alberti, Impact Publishers, Atascadero, CA, 2005

Chapter 3

BELIEVING

I CAN

SAVE HIM

Another basic human need: To matter in this world.

Being needed can make a woman feel valued, even when the person who needs her does harm to her. Their relationship gives her a purpose—to love him enough to heal his pain. Her partner tells a sad story about his horrible life, how no one has ever understood him, how everyone has let him down, how he was mistreated. She, being a nurturer, rushes in to "save" him. She wants to show him that the world is not a terrible place and that she will always stand steadfastly beside him.

Her partner reinforces this behavior as a way to hold on to her. He occasionally indulges her with kind treatment or gifts to support her belief that her efforts are not in vain, motivating her to continue to seek his undying devotion. Meanwhile, he is mentally keeping track of his "good deeds"; she owes him for his extra attention. She will pay for it when he returns to his former abusive behavior.

Along with feeling needed, she fears failing if the relationship falls apart. She has invested time and effort into trying to "fix" things. Even when the pain of the relationship becomes extreme, she hesitates to leave. To do so would mean not only that she wasted her time, but also that she would have to start over with someone new. One of her greatest fears is that her partner will change after she leaves and someone else will reap the reward of her effort. She lives between *if I can just hang on long enough, he will change* and *if I leave and he changes, I will miss out.*

Meanwhile, she is already missing out on the happy and peaceful life she deserves.

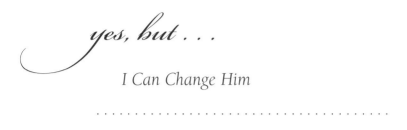

yes, but . . .

I Can Change Him

I am the only person I can change.

This relationship isn't a gothic romance where the hero is a misunderstood rebel waiting for me to transform his life. That's fiction. I'm not a miracle worker. It's misguided for me to think that I can change him.

My partner expects me to change to meet his expectations. Yet he won't seek help in the form of domestic violence therapy to change his behavior for my benefit. Hoping, praying, or pleading will not change his behavior. People make their own choices and do what works for them. Showering him with love will not stop the abuse. I can't love him into changing. Becoming a doormat or martyr will not make him love me or treat me any better. Although he may have told me repeatedly that he wants to stop hurting me, he hasn't. There is little hope for healing this relationship if he cannot, or will not, understand or respect my feelings.

I won't buy in to the hook that he "needs me" to help him change. He must make the effort to change himself, for himself. If he wants to change, there are resources available that can help him learn to make better choices. If he refuses to get help, he's not interested in healing the relationship.

If he does choose to attend therapy, I will use that time to work on my own issues. If he's serious about healing our relationship, he'll take responsibility for his actions and show a commitment to treatment. His therapist will determine his level of dedication to healing and will communicate with me directly about his progress.

Even if he gets professional help, I still have the option to leave. That is always an option. Leaving him is not an excuse for him to quit trying to change. Telling me that he can't make it without me is an attempt to continue to control me. I won't buy into it.

TRUTHS

- If he can't or will not understand or respect my feelings, it's unlikely that he'll change.
- If he truly wanted to stop being abusive, he'd do what it takes to make a permanent change.
- He is the only one who can make the choice to stop hurting me.
- I can make choices only for myself.
- I have the right to decide at any point that the relationship is over, no matter where he is in his recovery process.

ISSUES TO EXPLORE

1. My desire to "fix" my partner
2. Is it realistic to believe that I can change him?
3. My own control issues

I Can Save Him

. . . .

In my journal, I will examine the following questions:

~ *Why do I think he needs saving?*

~ *What do I think is threatening him?*

I can't save him from himself or his choices. He must save himself.

As long as I fight his battles and fix his mistakes, he'll never take responsibility for his own life.

It's self-defeating for me to become angry, frustrated with his life, or protective of him. Doing so only allows him to avoid being accountable for himself and gives the stress and responsibility for his current state to me. He'll have no desire to make the needed changes.

I can save only myself. If my partner doesn't take steps to change his behavior, I can choose to put an end to the abuse by planning carefully so my children and I can safely leave.

TRUTHS

- He must save himself.
- I'll fight my own battles and let him fight his.
- I have the power to save myself.

ISSUES TO EXPLORE

1. My desire to save him
2. How to stop carrying his emotions
3. How to cast off the responsibility I feel for his life

yes, but . . .

He Needs Me

or

He Can't Live without Me

. . . .

Saying he needs me is a powerful hook. I won't allow my desire to be important in someone's life override my need to take care of my children and myself.

He wants someone to

~ *make him feel important, worshipped, and adored*

~ *meet his every need regardless of the cost to me*

~ *cook and clean*

~ *provide sex*

~ *take responsibility for his destructive behavior*

I have tried to

~ *heal his past pain*

~ *restore his faith in the world as a good place*

~ *bring him to God*

As an adult, my partner can learn to take care of himself and reach out for professional help. I can't heal him or be everything to him. It's unhealthy for me to try to be all things to him at my expense.

My needs are important too.

I want a partner who

~ *listens to me*

~ *respects my feelings*

~ *encourages me to do the things I love*

~ *discusses problems calmly*

~ *negotiates differences*

~ *is my safe place to land*

~ *is supportive of my life, beliefs, and values*

~ *shares the household work*

Healthy relationships are a two-way street, where both partners' needs are valued. They both are responsible for loving, respecting, and cherishing each other. If his needs are paramount and mine are left unmet, I feel drained and empty. This is not a healthy relationship.

Telling me he needs me and threatening to commit suicide or kill me if I leave him is coercion. My partner intends to hold me in the relationship. I will take his threats seriously and seek help from people who are trained to deal with such threats and who can protect me. (See the Chart of Coercion on pages 205–206 for more information.)

TRUTHS

- I won't allow my need to feel important in someone's life override caring for my children and myself.
- I can't be everything to him, nor should I be.
- Both partners are responsible for loving, respecting, and cherishing each other.
- My needs are important.

ISSUES TO EXPLORE

1. My need to feel important in someone's life

2. The balance between caring for others and caring for myself

3. How to set and hold boundaries

4. Activities that will reenergize me

5. What traits I would want in a partner

yes, but . . .

I Have to Make This Work—I Don't Want to Be a Failure

Whether or not I took a vow, I don't have to feel like a failure or a fool if this relationship fails. I don't have to buy into shame. I can't make the relationship work by myself.

Leaving this relationship is a victory, not a failure. Although I may be afraid, humiliated, and embarrassed for being in an abusive relationship, if I choose to leave, I will reach out for help. By using the resources in my community, I can plan for and then safely remove myself (and my children) from this painful situation.

Leaving is difficult, so I won't allow myself to feel guilty if I return. I'm not a failure. I'm not disappointing my therapist or anyone else. This is my life and I must do what I need to do. It may take a few attempts to leave before I am able to stay out of this relationship. As I work through this, I will continue to grow stronger.

My partner plays a game with me when he dangles a carrot of hope that our relationship will improve. By his actions or words, he implies that if I change who I am, he will love me. His game is designed to keep me focused on him and to have him remain the center of my world. My partner doesn't plan to return the devotion that he demands. Without his cooperation, this relationship will never be what I hoped for.

Leaving a relationship filled with pain and abuse doesn't mean I'm a loser, a failure, or unlovable. It's a victory for me (and my children); having the strength and courage to leave, when the time is right, shows that I am putting our needs first.

TRUTHS

- I will reach out for help.
- Leaving an abusive relationship is a victory.

ISSUES TO EXPLORE

1. Reconsidering my understanding of success and failure
2. Owning my right to be treated with respect

yes, but . . .

I've Already Put So Much Energy into This Relationship That Would Go to Waste

. . . .

"It's never too late to turn around when you are headed down the wrong path."

OLD PROVERB

I can't force this relationship to become what I had hoped. My partner won't take the necessary steps to improve our life together. Yes, I have spent a considerable amount of time in this painful relationship, but continuing to stay with someone who is abusive and refuses to change is a waste of my precious time.

He tells me what I want to hear to keep me with him. If he really wanted to change, he would seek professional help and follow through. Though I want him to think our relationship is worth the effort, his actions show me differently.

I have made an effort to improve our relationship. Things haven't changed. My partner can't see beyond his own needs and wants. He lacks empathy for me.

I must decide what I will do next. Am I going to continue to waste my time with someone who won't change? Will I begin to make changes in my life that will lead me to safety?

I deserve a partner who treats me well because he loves me, not because I threaten to leave.

If the time I have invested in this relationship makes me stay, I'm teaching my children to put up with abuse. I want to teach them to stand up for themselves and maintain control of their lives.

If I leave, each passing year will decrease the percentage of my life I gave to this person. This experience need not define my life.

After I heal, I may decide to seek a new relationship with someone who meets my needs—a good investment of my valuable time.

TRUTHS

- It's never too late to turn around when you're heading down the wrong path.
- His actions have nothing to do with my worth or value.
- I can't force this relationship to become what I had hoped.
- I won't waste one more moment of my precious time with an abusive partner.
- I deserve a partner who treats me well because he wants to, not because he is afraid of losing me.
- I will teach my children to stand up for themselves and maintain control of their own lives.

- This relationship will only be a small percentage of my whole life and will not define my life.

ISSUES TO EXPLORE

1. Why letting go is so hard
2. What I want my new path to look like
3. The kind of person I want to spend my valuable time with

yes, but . . .

*I've Already Put So Much Energy
into This Relationship—If I Leave,
Someone Else Will Benefit
from My Hard Work*

. . . .

People do what works for them. Unless my partner seeks professional help and learns new ways of relating, he will abuse his next partner. If he refuses to get help to save our relationship, he will refuse to change for his next partner as well. If my leaving does lead him to change, so be it. The bottom line is—he won't change his ways if I stay only to prevent him from being with someone else. Doing so would be trapping myself in this misery. I have to face it: This relationship will never be what I had hoped for.

If I stay in this relationship, he'll think I'm willing to put up with the abuse. Staying means I'm giving up the life I could have for someone who isn't interested in giving anything back to me.

It's important to model self-care and self-respect for my children. This will benefit them and their own future relationships.

TRUTHS

- This relationship will never be the one I hoped it would be.
- Staying in an abusive relationship only wastes my time.

- It's important that I show my children how to respect and care for themselves.
- This is not the only man I can love.

ISSUES TO EXPLORE

1. Letting go of the relationship
2. Maintaining my self-worth
3. Understanding that this relationship doesn't define me

Chapter 4

SACRIFICING

MY SELF

Some women in relationships with abusive partners come from families who did not or could not nurture their spirits. As these women grew up, they understood that the people they cared about saw little or no value in them, leaving them with low self-esteem and the misconception that they were unworthy of love and care.

A woman's longing for an intimate connection, however, does not cease. When she meets a man who is skilled at manipulating others, he will dangle love before her in such a way that she may become willing to sacrifice anything, including her authentic self, for him.

Being perceptive, she quickly learns his likes, dislikes, and needs. She strives to be who he wants her to be, and to create the lifestyle and home her partner desires, hoping he will be grateful and show her love in return. However, with an abusive man who feels no empathy for others, these efforts to win his love are fruitless. Such a man is a taker; he gives only when there is a payoff for him or he perceives a threat that will disrupt his world. Neither she nor the home will ever be good enough in his eyes. He will always find fault with something, or make up something, brainwashing her into believing that she is useless and incompetent. Her self-esteem sinks even more. Traumatized by him as well as by other disappointing relationships in her life, she comes to feel that she "owes" her partner devotion because he chose her; at this point, she considers herself lucky to have anyone. Or she might be from a generation that expects women to stay quiet and just accept anything that happens in the home.

The longer she stays in such a relationship, the more she loses and sacrifices her inner being. Indeed, she knows his needs, likes, and dislikes more than her own. So keyed into him, she may know him better than he knows himself. She often sees behind his bravado façade to his fear of powerlessness and weakness. Being compassionate, she doesn't want to exacerbate his suffering; she seeks to ease it.

As the victim of abuse loses her independence and self, her partner gains the upper hand in the relationship. Other factors that may help him maintain control and manipulate her further include various religious and cultural beliefs and practices.

In Bill Moyer's documentary *Beyond Our Differences,* the Dalai Lama stresses that the foundation of all religions includes the principles of love, compassion, forgiveness, and tolerance.[16] However, religious tenets are sometimes misused in an effort to prove women as lesser people. An abuser is often an expert at interpreting religious writings to support his desires at the expense of his partner. He will point out her responsibility as a wife while failing to live up to his own responsibility as a husband. The abuser concocts a toxic faith[17] that serves him rather than God. (Note: In this chapter, the word *God* is used as a generic term for our higher power, be it God, Allah, Yahweh, Buddha, or whatever name used by your faith.) The truth is that helping her partner, or anyone, should never hurt her.

She can also misunderstand teachings and not hold her partner accountable for his behavior. Intending to keep her wedding-day promises, she might believe her husband is second to God or that the ill-treatment is karma for a past life's sin. Therefore, she must accept the abuse.

The omnipotent beings of all faiths clearly call for a peaceful, nurturing, and loving relationship within marriage as well as all partnerships.

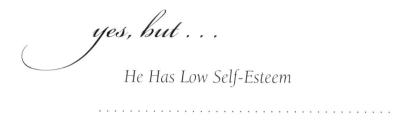

yes, but . . .

He Has Low Self-Esteem

I can't repair anyone else's self-image. I can be encouraging and honest, but I can't heal someone else. He must help himself.

He can rebuild his self-esteem through therapy. If he doesn't believe in therapy or going into treatment, that's his choice. He chooses to remain the same.

If he says he depends on me and he can't live without me, I'll recognize that statement as a hook designed to maintain the current situation. I'll read "Yes, but . . . He Needs Me, or He Can't Live Without Me" (pages 104–106) to remind myself that he says these things only to keep me from leaving him.

TRUTHS

- I am the only person I can fix.
- He makes choices about his own life.
- I make choices about my life.

ISSUES TO EXPLORE

1. Healthy versus unhealthy needs
2. What are dependency needs?
3. Setting self-protecting boundaries around my giving

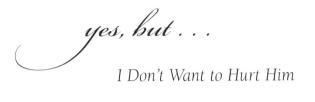

I Don't Want to Hurt Him

. . . .

It's his actions that are causing me to consider leaving him. He is responsible for any hurt he feels as a result of his behavior. After weighing my options, if I decide to leave, it is not an act of retribution, but one of self-care. It is not selfish to protect myself from harm.

Respecting myself means that I don't allow others to hurt me. If I stay with my partner, he'll continue to abuse me because people continue to do what has always benefited them.

TRUTHS

- Having respect for myself means I won't let other people continue to harm me.
- I am not responsible for his pain; he is.

ISSUES TO EXPLORE

1. Assessing the cost of this relationship
2. Overcoming guilt
3. Self-care
4. Holding my partner accountable for his actions

Suggested reading:

"The Bridge," in *Friedman's Fables* by Edwin H. Friedman, Guilford Press, New York, 1990

yes, but . . .

Everyone Else in His Life Has Let Him Down—I Am All He Has

. . . .

I won't buy this claim. When he tells me that no one has ever really loved him, it taps into my desire to be the hero in his life. Such statements are hooks used to hold me in this relationship. They trigger my compassion and bring out the martyr in me. I will no longer be a martyr.

If I make him my "project," he won't take responsibility for his own well-being. My overinvolvement hinders his recovery. It's his job to heal himself. If he truly wants to end the pain, he will get professional help.

In my journal, I will address the hooks he uses to make me feel sorry for him and develop a healthy response to his comments and complaints.

TRUTHS

- He is responsible for saving himself.
- As long as I'm willing to try to save him, he will not take responsibility for his own well-being.
- I will not be a martyr or a doormat.

ISSUES TO EXPLORE

1. How to stop being a martyr
2. Guilt
3. Healthy versus unhealthy dependency
4. How he has let me down

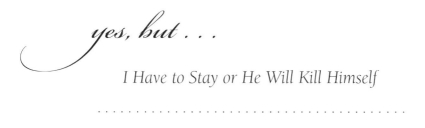

yes, but . . .

I Have to Stay or He Will Kill Himself

. . . .

This is coercion designed to hold me in the relationship. He may say that he is going to commit suicide to scare me. I will take his threats seriously. If he is in immediate danger, I will call 911. If he is not in immediate danger, I will report his threats to professionals who are equipped to handle persons with emotional problems.

I don't want him to commit suicide, but if he does, it is his choice; it is not my fault. Coercion and threats won't keep me in an unhealthy relationship.

I can only make choices for myself. I can't fix my partner. If he wants to heal, he must take the necessary steps. His actions are his choice.

TRUTHS

- I can remove myself from an unhealthy relationship.
- My partner is responsible for his own behavior.
- My partner's suicide threats may be desperate attempts to manipulate me. However, I will take my partner's suicide threats seriously and report them to someone who is trained to help.

ISSUES TO EXPLORE

1. How guilt has held me in the relationship
2. Other "hooks" he uses that are coercive, threatening, or guilt-creating
3. How to respond to coercion and threats

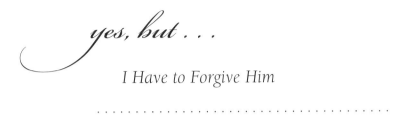

I Have to Forgive Him

"Those who have been victimized for years, who have been told that they are wrong for objecting to their victimization, need to remember that forgiveness is compatible with asking someone to stop doing bad things to us, to others or to themselves."

ROBERT D. ENRIGHT, PH.D., *FORGIVENESS IS A CHOICE*

Eventually, I will consider the possibility of forgiving him. I don't need to do that right now. First, I will take care of my immediate needs. When I am ready to explore the issue of forgiveness, I will remember that forgiving is not condoning or excusing. I will seek guidance from a therapist or support group when I'm ready to start the process of forgiveness.

Forgiving him doesn't mean I have to

~ *stay with him*
~ *continue to put myself (and my children) in a position to be mistreated*
~ *give him another chance*

Forgiveness and reconciliation are two different things. Forgiveness doesn't require me to stay or return to the relationship. (See Robert Enright's interview online for more information. See page xiii in the front of this book for instructions on accessing the interview.)

Forgiveness neither wipes away the sin as if it never happened, nor says that the behavior was okay. I won't forget what happened. That would be impossible.

To forgive means the following:

~ *I acknowledge that his behavior is terrible.*

~ *I hold my partner responsible for his actions and words.*

~ *I refuse to allow him to treat me in that manner again.*

~ *I can remove myself (and our children) from the relationship.*

~ *I can move on with my life.*

Forgiveness takes time. My partner's standard routine is to pressure me to forgive him immediately after he says he's sorry. If he's truly repentant, he will take full responsibility for his actions and respect my need to process my feelings in my own time frame. He will also take steps to change his behavior.

It is my right to work through this issue at my own pace. Being contrite yet insisting that I am cruel for not forgiving him immediately is his way of pressuring me into saying I forgive him so we can go back to the way things were—the way he likes it. History has shown me that shortly after I forgive him, he will return to his bad behavior.

TRUTHS

- Before I consider forgiving him, I will concentrate on my (and my children's) immediate needs.

- True forgiveness takes time and isn't easy.

- I can forgive him and still end the relationship.

- Forgiveness acknowledges the terribleness of the incident and does not excuse it.

- Forgiveness is compatible with asking him to stop doing bad things to me, to others, or to himself.

ISSUES TO EXPLORE

1. What it means to forgive
2. The right time for me to consider forgiving him

Suggested reading:

Forgiveness Is a Choice: A Step-by-Step Process for Resolving Anger and Restoring Hope by Robert D. Enright, APA LifeTools, Washington DC, 2001

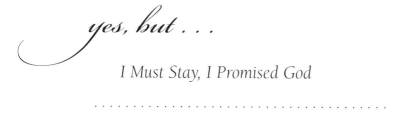

I Must Stay, I Promised God

All religions teach the basic principles of love and compassion. They abhor violence and advise us to treat one another as we would like to be treated.

God calls for partners in intimate relationships to earn each other's respect and adoration. One cannot demand or force these feelings. Physical or verbal attacks breed fear, not love and respect.

Marriage is a covenant that two people make between God and each other in which they promise to love and cherish each other and live in peace. People who abuse their partners break that covenant.

As a loving parent, I would never want my child hit, punched, kicked, thrown against the wall, berated, humiliated, or worse. None of the above acts of violence will make my child a "better" person.

In the same manner, God, who loves me more perfectly than I love my children, doesn't want or expect me to suffer any kind of abuse or live in fear.

I have a God-given purpose on this earth. My purpose isn't to be a physical or emotional punching bag for someone else.

God would not expect me to tolerate abuse. Because God loves me, God wants my partner to cherish me as I develop my gifts and achieve my purpose in life.

Though I may have promised to obey or submit to my partner, he doesn't have the right to take God's place in my life, or to abuse me. My partner is twisting the intention of our vows when he uses them to give himself total power over me or to justify the abuse.

If my partner creates chaos and fear in our home in addition to one or more of the following actions, he is trying to stand in the way of my relationship with God. This is a form of abuse. Such actions include:

~ *Preventing me from attending the worship place of my choice*

~ *Demeaning my beliefs*

~ *Forcing me to do things against my beliefs (For more information on spiritual abuse, see* What Is Abuse? *on pages 196–197.)*

My partner's relationship with God is his responsibility. I may be a part of God's plan by setting an example of living my life in the way God would choose. However, it is misguided to believe that I can "save" my partner. If I tolerate abuse, I am allowing him to believe it is okay to treat people this way. It is not. Leaving him may be exactly what my partner needs to awaken to God's purpose for his life.

Sacrificing myself by staying with a man who abuses me doesn't make me holier or more loved by God. I am not letting God down by ending the relationship. God loves me whether I stay or leave.

I can seek help and support from my house of worship. However, I'll carefully evaluate the leaders' views on domestic violence. If I receive messages from them that say one or more of the following, I will seek a

new worship place where all members and leaders treat me as a worthy
child loved by God:

~ *You are not praying hard enough or correctly.*

~ *This relationship is your cross to bear.*

~ *The abuse is payback for sins in a previous life.*

~ *You must submit to your husband's demands.*

~ *You are exaggerating.*

I can make a good choice now that can free me from suffering, closing
the door to abuse and opening the door of possibilities for me to have the
fulfilling and happy life I deserve.

TRUTHS

* I become a better person by building a relationship
  with God and fulfilling my divine purpose.

* Only I am responsible for making me a better person.

* God does not want me to remain in an abusive
  relationship.

* God wants me to protect myself and my children.

ISSUES TO EXPLORE

1. My fear of controlling my own life

2. My belief that I must submit to a man who abuses me

3. How to uncover my God-given gifts

Chapter 5

BLAMING MYSELF

FOR HIS BEHAVIOR—

BELIEVING I

DESERVE IT

In today's busy world, creating a life of balance is a goal for many women. Victims of abuse are no different; they strive to do their best in various roles—wife, homemaker, parent, and, if their partner allows, career woman.

Unlike nonvictims, the woman in an abusive relationship lives with a partner who demands perfection—as defined by him. Falling short of his demands triggers a violent episode. Because she wasn't able to live up to his definition of perfection, under his pressure, she may buy into her partner's claim that she deserves the abuse. This begins a vicious cycle:

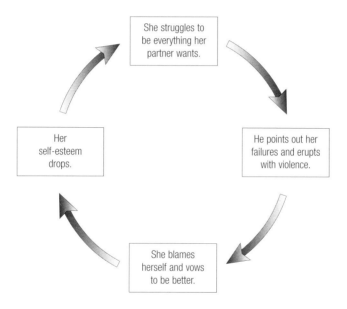

Some women are quick to accept responsibility for their partner's bad behavior in other ways. She may tell herself that if she could just love him enough, he would change. She feels guilty when it doesn't work. She hoped she could make a difference in his life. When she can't, her self-esteem plummets.

In an attempt to feel she has some control over the situation, she may take steps to become prettier, thinner, smarter, or a better housekeeper, or to change whatever he's criticized about her. She's sure that change will return their relationship to what it was when he thought she was his ideal mate. But despite her best efforts, he continues to criticize her actions and her physical appearance. The more she internalizes his disapproval, the lower her self-esteem drops. The messages in her head now tell her she is worthless and deserves the abuse. Her partner, who planted those messages, is all too happy to confirm this false belief.

In the cycle of abuse, the period leading up to the battering is thick with unbearable tension. The woman, so keyed into his demeanor, feels the buildup and knows a violent episode is inevitable. Deep in the agony and fear of not knowing when he will strike out, she seeks to relieve the pressure. She deliberately sets him off. It may be because she can't bear the anguish another moment and just wants to get to the other side. Or, more important to her, she knows the children will be home from school shortly. She wants the incident to be over so the children won't hear or witness it. Whatever her reasoning, deliberately triggering his abuse reinforces her false belief that she is responsible for it. Her partner will most certainly point out the fact that she started it. In reality, she is in no way responsible for his abusive behavior. He has cornered her into giving him a reason to hurt her. The choice whether to hit or not is his alone.

yes, but . . .

If Only I Could Just Love Him Enough, He Would Change

It's not possible to love him into change. I can fill his Emotional Bank Account with kind words, encouragement, and trust, but I can't heal the damage from his past.[18] He needs to work with a trained professional and take responsibility for healing his own pain. He is the only one who can do that work. My efforts to help and my love for him will not change him.

I don't have to be subservient or a willing victim to prove my love for him. And doing so certainly won't make him love me any more or treat me any better. If I continue to tolerate his abusive behavior, he doesn't need to change.

Helping him shouldn't cause me pain and suffering. It's time for me to learn how to love and honor myself.

I'm worth loving and worth treating right.

I'll teach my children how to love and honor themselves.

TRUTHS

- Loving him won't change him or stop him from abusing me.
- Giving my partner support should not lead to hurt and suffering.
- If I sacrifice my health and well-being for this person, I don't show honor to myself.

ISSUES TO EXPLORE

1. What keeps me tied to this man
2. How to love and honor myself

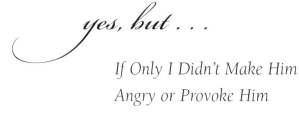

yes, but . . .

If Only I Didn't Make Him Angry or Provoke Him

. . . .

Even if I make him angry, his response is his choice. A dusty house or late dinner doesn't give him the right to harm me physically or emotionally. People in healthy relationships talk about a problem, they don't berate each other or become violent.

He's trying to blame me for his actions when he says I make him so angry he can't help himself. Abuse isn't an anger issue. It's a power and control issue. I refuse to take responsibility for his bad behavior. He's making a choice to be abusive. If he can choose to hurt me, he can choose not to hurt me.

I will weigh the situation carefully, then I'll decide if I must tolerate his behavior or leave.

TRUTHS

- I won't accept blame for his bad behavior.
- Abusive behavior is a choice.
- In healthy relationships, partners talk through their problems without harsh words or physical violence.
- I choose whether or not to put up with his behavior.

ISSUES TO EXPLORE

1. How to change my role in the cycle of violence
2. How to hold him accountable for his abusive behavior

yes, but . . .

If Only I Were More Attractive/ Thinner/Smarter/More Interesting/ a Better Communicator/More Fun

. . . .

None of the above has anything to do with his bad behavior.

No matter how beautiful, thin, intelligent, interesting, or fun I am, it won't stop him from abusing me. My looks and other characteristics have nothing to do with his choices. I have no control over his actions.

Calling me fat and making other comments about my body is demeaning. I am beautiful just as I am. Even if I am trying to lose weight, his remarks are detrimental to my efforts; he wants me to fail so I will feel bad about myself. He's intentionally messing with my mind and undermining my progress. (For more information on emotional abuse, see What Is Abuse? on pages 195–196.)

I am intelligent, capable, interesting, insightful, and personable. He calls me stupid and boring to make me feel inferior and make himself feel superior. He wants me to believe I deserve to be berated and abused. He's trying to destroy my self-esteem so I won't feel confident enough to walk away.

He pretends I'm confused and twists my words around when I try to discuss my concerns with him. It is his way of making me feel stupid and, therefore, ending the conversation. His intention is to keep the situation as is.

No matter how spontaneous and free I act, it won't stop his cruel behavior. He'll find fault with me for being too spontaneous and free.

Fun is a relative term. Each individual defines it. What he thinks is fun may not be fun to me, and I have told him this repeatedly. Yet he persists in trying to goad me into situations and berates me when I refuse to participate. In healthy relationships, partners don't expect each other to do things they find uncomfortable or life-threatening. These requests show his lack of respect for me.

TRUTHS

- My looks and other characteristics have nothing to do with his bad behavior.
- Partners in healthy relationships don't ask each other to engage in uncomfortable or life-threatening behavior.
- I won't accept the blame for his bad behavior.
- I won't allow him to bully or cajole me into anything.
- I am intelligent, beautiful, and capable.
- I am worthy of a happy, healthy relationship.
- I have a right to be who I am.

ISSUES TO EXPLORE

1. Self-image versus body image
2. Self-acceptance
3. Trusting myself

yes, but . . .

I Made My Bed,
Now I Have to Lie in It

. . . .

"You did what you knew how to do. When you knew better,
you did better."

MAYA ANGELOU

My partner romanced me into this relationship with smooth talk and lies. I trusted him. Though my trust was misplaced, trusting people is not wrong. I may have invested a lot of time and energy into this relationship, but it's not too late to make a change. I will not punish myself for the rest of my life for loving the wrong person, nor will I make the mistake of allowing him to continue controlling me.

My actions now show my children how to set boundaries and make life-changing improvements.

TRUTHS

- I did what I knew how to do. Now that I know better, I will do better.
- By standing up for myself, I am showing my children how to establish boundaries and make life-changing improvements.

ISSUES TO EXPLORE

1. The need to punish myself for something I had no control over
2. Trusting others with both eyes open
3. Protecting myself

yes, but . . .

*I Never Do Anything Right—I Always
Let Him Down/Disappoint Him/Say and
Do the Wrong Thing/Blow It*

· ·

*"When we let ourselves be defined in our own minds by
our worst moments instead of our best ones, we learn to
think of ourselves as people who never get it right, rather
than as capable people who make an occasional, thoroughly
human mistake."*

HAROLD S. KUSHNER, *HOW GOOD DO WE HAVE TO BE?*

He demands that I be "perfect." He sets the bar so high that it's impossible to
meet his expectations. Should I come close, he'll raise the bar to keep me off
balance, busy, and focused on him instead of on how he is treating me.

No one is perfect. No one has the right to determine what I need to
"fix" about myself. I'll stop spending my energy trying to please him and
begin working on ways to improve my self-esteem. I am capable. I do many
things right and I am good enough just the way I am. He is messing with
my mind when he

~ *criticizes everything I do or say*

~ *tells me I have broken a rule I never knew existed*

~ *changes the rules at his own whim*

~ *tells me that I could have had it right if I had just done something else*

~ *blames me for things I didn't do*

~ *projects his shortcomings onto me—calling me a slob or accusing
me of having an affair*

~ *hides my possessions so I think I've misplaced them*

~ *insists that I said or did something that I didn't say or do*

~ *twists my words to change their meaning*

In my journal, I'll list other ways he tries to convince me that I'm losing my mind.

My partner may also try to make others think I'm crazy. Though I have no control over what others think of me, I will continue to be who I am and hope that others see my partner's game.

Even if my partner calls my opinions or ideas stupid, I am entitled to them and may express my thoughts and feelings. No one has the right to tell me what I should think or how I should feel.

TRUTHS

- I will focus on my successes, not my occasional failures.
- I refuse to buy into his "crazy-making" attempts (messing with my mind).
- I'll focus on building my self-esteem.
- I'm capable of controlling my own life.
- I have a right to my own ideas and feelings.

ISSUES TO EXPLORE

1. My desire to be perfect
2. The fear of making a mistake
3. Ways that I am a lovable person
4. What's right about me

Chapter 6

BLAMING OUTSIDE

FORCES FOR HIS

BEHAVIOR

An abuser will go to great lengths to cast responsibility for his abusive behavior elsewhere, creating smoke and mirrors to do so and blaming others for his actions. His main target is his partner. But he also blames people outside their home. He may declare that his boss, coaches, or professors are unreasonable and put too much pressure on him, or that her family treats him poorly. He may even declare he is in a spiritual struggle with the devil who makes him abuse her. This is a tactic to garner sympathy and pull the victim's role away from the real victim—his partner.

Having fallen prey to the Stockholm Syndrome, the real victim may have deep sympathy for her partner. Since he has placed the responsibility for making his life easy squarely on her shoulders, she feels the pressure to manage everyone and everything around him. She may be able to manage the children, chores, and house, but she has no control over the people he encounters in the outside world. Nor does she have control over his use of alcohol or other drugs.

When her partner drinks too much, gambles, does drugs, or has affairs, she accepts his claim that his daily stress is the cause. She's sure if his stress level decreased, his addiction would go away. Meanwhile, she pays the price for his addictions and rage.

yes, but . . .

If Only He Could Quit Drinking/
Doing Drugs/Gambling/
Having Affairs

. . . .

"Here's the secret about addicts: They are often incredibly seductive. They can be the most charismatic people in the room—the most fun to be with, and seemingly the most spiritually alive and sensitive of souls . . . What I now know that I didn't understand during my relationship is that an addict is more attached to the addiction than to anything or anyone else. It was an illusion that my partner was spiritually alive or sensitive. It was exactly the opposite. He was spiritually dead and fully cut off from his ability to care about me or anyone else in his life."

Dr. Robin L. Smith, *Lies at the Altar*

He doesn't abuse me because he uses or has a problem with alcohol or other drugs. He abuses me because he chooses to. The alcohol and drugs may make it easier to act on his intention, but they don't cause the behavior. As long as he refuses to make better choices, he'll continue to abuse me, whether he's high or sober.

His gambling puts my children's future and me at risk.

His seeing other women is degrading and humiliating for me. Someone who loves me would never put me in this position. Neither would they risk giving me a sexually transmitted disease. His affairs put my life at stake and could deprive my children of their mother.

There is help for those who want to stop their addiction. He must make the choice to stop. I can't make him change.

TRUTHS

- Staying sober doesn't mean he'll stop abusing me.
- Alcohol and other drugs don't make a person abusive.
- It's his responsibility to address his addictions and their cause.
- I'll hold him responsible for his choices.

ISSUES TO EXPLORE

1. What *enabling* means
2. What *codependency* means
3. Ways to stop being an enabler

yes, but . . .

If Only His Boss/Teacher/
Coach Wouldn't Put Him Under
So Much Stress

. . . .

My partner is the only one responsible for his behavior. Other people in his life do not drive him to be abusive. Even if he changes jobs or quits school, he will still abuse me. While stress may increase his tendency to violence, he still makes the final choice. It's my partner's job to address the stress in his life and to learn to deal with it in a healthy and appropriate manner.

TRUTHS

- My partner is the only one responsible for his behavior.
- Stress doesn't make a person abusive.
- It's his responsibility to address stress in his life and to learn to deal with it in a healthy and appropriate manner.

ISSUES TO EXPLORE

1. Understanding that others do not cause the abuse
2. How I manage stress/ways to de-stress

yes, but . . .

The Devil Made Him Do It

When my partner is contrite and moans about his struggle against Satan to stop his behavior, he is only laying his responsibility for his actions on yet another source—in this case, Satan. He does this to hook into my sympathy and keep me in the relationship.

To stop me from leaving him, he may also make false claims that God has "healed" him. In reality, God's healing will come for my partner when he begins work with a qualified therapist. I will not fall for his claims of conversion or miraculous healing. Even if he currently is or becomes a follower of God, I don't have to stay in this relationship.

God gives us the right to make good choices or bad choices. My prayers and hopes will not change my partner's right to make bad choices. Only my partner can change himself.

TRUTHS

- People of faith take responsibility for their actions and treat others as they would like to be treated.
- Neither God nor Satan is responsible for my partner's behavior.
- I will be cautious of my partner's claim to have "found God" and been "healed."
- Even if he adopts a faith, I don't have to remain in this relationship.

ISSUES TO EXPLORE

1. My belief about God's role in solving problems in my life

2. The different ways that my partner casts blame for his behavior elsewhere

yes, but . . .

If Only My Family and Friends Would Treat Him Better or Be More Accepting and Accommodating

No matter how my family chooses to treat my partner, his response to that treatment is his choice. As much as I'd like everyone to love one another and treat each other with respect, it isn't going to happen. My partner's actions may well be the reason my family responds to him with disapproval.

I won't protect or excuse someone who behaves badly. I won't blame my family for my partner's bad behavior. His actions are not a reflection of my family or me.

By trying to convince me that my family is unworthy of our attention, by causing conflicts whenever we are with my family, and by taking out his anger toward my family on me, he hopes to keep me away from my family. He uses my fear of conflict to isolate me, building a wall between my family and me. If he succeeds, I lose an important part of my support system. This gives my partner more power and control in my life. I will not let him sever my relationship with my family or friends.

I don't deserve someone who acts out and alienates others. I don't deserve a partner who humiliates me in front of my family or friends. I deserve a partner who treats my family and me with respect.

TRUTHS

- I can't control other people's actions or feelings, nor should I be punished for them.
- I will not allow my partner to isolate me from my family and friends.
- I deserve someone in my life who respects both me and my family.

ISSUES TO EXPLORE

1. My fear of conflict
2. How to handle conflict
3. What I think a healthy relationship with extended family looks like
4. How to talk with my family and friends about what is really going on in my life
5. How my family and friends can safely help me if I chose to leave

Chapter 7

ACCEPTING

MALE

PRIVILEGE

Despite great strides in the women's movement, many myths about male privilege and superiority persist, such as men are smarter, more capable, and deserve to have their sexual desires met. In the United States, women have lived under male-set expectations for most of their history. Women did not earn the right to vote until 1920. After World War II when the men returned home, many women were removed from the jobs they did efficiently to make room for the men in the workplace. Not very long ago (the 1950s), a woman couldn't open a bank account without her husband's permission. Many of our schools still struggle to provide girls and women with an equal education.

In the work world today, women earn about 75 percent of what men earn in the same job with the same education and experience.[19] Women are still trying to attain equality and dispel old views. James B. Nelson, in his book *Embodiment,* argues that until women behave like men in leadership roles, they won't be respected as leaders. The "I'm the boss, do as I say" authoritarian style of management has become so ingrained as the preferred method of leadership that other styles, though effective, aren't accepted in many organizations. Some executives still view women's strength in relational management as a sign of weakness.

One of the strongest hooks that holds a woman in an abusive relationship is her lack of financial resources. Her partner controls the money under the pretext that as a man, he is more capable. He either keeps her from working or takes charge of her earnings. If she brought any assets into the relationship, he makes sure his name is included on her deeds or accounts. It's not unusual for a controlling man to siphon his wife's funds into his personal hidden account.

It's not surprising that some women accept male privilege. Many grew up with these myths. Their dad was the "king of the castle" and their brothers were the favored children with important roles. Young girls were expected to sit on a pedestal and look pretty. Wives were expected to submit to their husband. And men were expected to be the main breadwinner of the family.

The view that males and their needs are superior becomes especially evident during the teenage years. Almost any teenage girl will attest that "guys need sex" and some feel pressured to "put out" in order to get or hold on to a boyfriend. Surveys show girls as young as sixth graders perform oral sex on demand to get a boyfriend.

For decades, girls have heard the following:

~ *"If you love me you will . . ."*

~ *"You did it with him, why not me?"*

~ *"Everyone else is doing it. What's wrong with you?"*

~ *"Obviously, you're not mature."*

~ *"You're too uptight."*

~ *"You're frigid."*

The media also plays a role in spreading myths about lopsided relationships and sexuality. "Bad boys" are portrayed as hot and exciting and "nice guys" as boring. As a result, young women may seek the excitement they see in movies and music videos and mistake the cycle of abuse for passion: the highs of the honeymoon period, anxiety during the tension building, the incident of violence, followed by the thrill of the honeymoon period returning. This "thrill" comes at the expense of the women's self-esteem.

Date rape is common, but here again the myth of male superiority is often seen. In court, fingers point to what she wore and why she invited him into her dorm room or apartment, or why she went with him to his. Attorneys for the defendant often blame and revictimize the victim during a trial. Did she lead him on? Is she trying to make trouble for him because she changed her mind after they had sex? Is she seeking revenge because he didn't call her the next day? Look at the sexy clothes she wore; she was asking for it. She wasn't a virgin, so what's the big deal? Again, society reinforces these myths and judges women by male concepts, blaming her for his bad behavior, making him the victim. No one suggests a man deserves the mugging because he walked down a street late at night. A woman faces the questions: "Why were you there? How could you be so stupid to do that?" It's no surprise when women refuse to press charges.

The truth is that men are not animals, and their needs and desires are not more important than women's. Both men and women have the power of choice and are accountable for their choices. In healthy relationships, partners are equally attracted to each other and develop a sexual relationship that is consensual and respectful. They also regard each other as true partners, where each has an equal voice in major decisions and one doesn't have to defer constantly to the other.

yes, but . . .

Men Should Make All the Decisions

. . . .

In healthy relationships, partners discuss and agree on major decisions such as

~ *the purchase of a house, car, or other expensive items*

~ *where they will live*

~ *how many children they will have*

They decide together how to raise and discipline the children. Both parties are aware of and have input into all finances. Together they have agreed on a plan for the future.

I have a right to make decisions that affect my life and to participate equally in decisions that affect our life together. I also have a right to all the pertinent information before I weigh in on such decisions. Having to ask questions doesn't mean I'm stupid. It means I'm interested in learning more. The more information I have, the better my decision will be.

I am capable of making good decisions and will respect my intuition and nurture it. Not all my decisions will be good. I won't beat myself up for mistakes. I'll learn from them and go on.

TRUTHS

- I have a right to make decisions that will affect my life.
- I have the right to an equal say in decisions that affect our life together.

- When I make mistakes, I will learn from them and go on.
- Asking questions before making a decision is wise.
- In a healthy relationship, partners make major decisions and purchases together.

ISSUES TO EXPLORE

1. Trusting my instincts
2. Forgiving my mistakes
3. My view of male privilege

yes, but . . .

Men Should Control All the Money and Property

or

Men Should Earn More Money Than Women

· ·

The need to control all the finances and property is his way of maintaining power over me. In a healthy relationship, these items are under joint ownership.

Even if I'm not interested in money management, it's important that I know our financial situation and am equally involved in deciding how we save and spend our money.

For a secure future, couples save a portion of their earnings. Another portion goes to pay living expenses. In addition, each partner has a reasonable amount of income to use at his or her discretion. Both partners are aware of all living expenses and income.

In a healthy relationship, a man is not offended if his partner's income exceeds his.

Financial experts recommend that each partner establish his or her own credit history and have an individual bank account and credit card.

My children and I deserve fair treatment. If I decide to leave my marriage, I will hire a skilled attorney to negotiate the financial settlement of my divorce.

TRUTHS

- In a healthy relationship, both partners are aware of all living expenses and income.
- Both partners should have a reasonable portion of income to use at their own discretion.
- In an equal partnership, both persons make financial decisions together.
- If I leave my marriage, my children and I deserve fair treatment in a divorce settlement.

ISSUES TO EXPLORE

1. How to protect myself financially
2. My current financial situation
3. My personal beliefs about money and love

Suggested reading:

Make Money, Not Excuses: Wake Up, Take Charge, and Overcome Your Financial Fears Forever by Jean Chatzky, Three Rivers Press, New York, 2008

Suze Orman's 2009 Action Plan by Suze Orman, Spiegel and Grau, New York, 2008

Women and Money: Owning the Power to Control Your Destiny by Suze Orman, Spiegel and Grau, New York, 2007

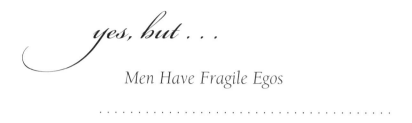

yes, but . . .

Men Have Fragile Egos

This is a myth. Men's egos are no more fragile than women's.

If demanding that he treat me with love and respect hurts his ego, so be it. In a healthy relationship, neither partner is in a "step-down position" (ranked as less important) to make the other feel good or worthy. His behavior is dehumanizing me and turning me into a possession. This is not okay.

We are each responsible for our own ego and what we choose to believe about ourselves.

TRUTHS

- Men's egos are no more fragile than women's.
- We are each responsible for our own ego.

ISSUES TO EXPLORE

1. Debunking the myths of male psychology and socialization
2. How to have difficult conversations with a partner

yes, but . . .

Men Don't Know How to Express Love

or

It's Just the Way Men Are

. . . .

"In authentic relating, each person is genuinely concerned for the other."

LEO BUSCAGLIA, *LOVING EACH OTHER*

No one person can meet all of the needs of another. (That's where friends, family, and professions come in.) However, in a healthy relationship, partners are open about their needs within the relationship and do their best to meet each other's needs. If I have told my partner how I want love expressed, and it is a reasonable request (for example, time, attention, hugs), his response shows me where I stand with him.

Within a committed relationship, someone who loves me will be happy to share hugs and kisses, make love, use kind words, encourage me, and show emotional support. Denying me these basic needs is his way of holding the power and control in the relationship.

If he only touches me when he wants sex, he's intentionally denying me closeness and a show of genuine caring. His intention is to make me so hungry for personal touch that I won't ever refuse to have sex with him. Withholding nonsexual touching and closeness is a way he demonstrates power over me. (For more information on sexual abuse, see What Is Abuse? on page 197.)

All people are unique individuals. We all choose who we want to be and how we treat others. Saying "That's just the way men are" is a male myth that allows men to not require any better of themselves. My partner treats me this way because he can. He lacks empathy and is not concerned about my feelings and needs. As long as I'm willing to put up with it, he'll continue to use this myth to justify his behavior.

TRUTHS

- In healthy relationships, partners do their best to meet each other's needs.
- In healthy relationships, each person is genuinely concerned for the other.
- We all choose who we want to be and how we will treat others.

ISSUES TO EXPLORE

1. Expressions of love
2. My preferences for affection
3. Other male myths

yes, but . . .

It's Okay for Him to Demand or Force Me to Have Sex

. . . .

Demanding sex is about power and control, not love and intimacy. If I have sex because I'm afraid what will happen if I say no to my partner, it's the same as being forced. People in healthy relationships respect each other's feelings. I have a right to say no. Whether married or not, forced or coerced sex is rape. (For more information on sexual abuse, see What Is Abuse? on page 197.)

TRUTHS

- Whether married or not, forced sex is always rape.
- I have the right to say no to my partner's sexual advances.

ISSUES TO EXPLORE

1. My level of fear
2. Building a mutually satisfying, nonabusive sexual relationship

Chapter 8

GIVING UP ON

MYSELF

After constant abuse, a woman has a low opinion of herself. From her perspective, the person who is the closest to her has verified that as is, she is not lovable. *What happened?* she asks herself. He used to think she was terrific, and they got along so well. She wonders what she can do to return the relationship to that state. She's willing to change anything about herself to make her partner happy. Then, she thinks, he won't lose his temper and berate or harm her.

Because an abuser's intention is to keep her off balance, whatever change she makes will not be good enough for him. All along he has been creating chaos in her life, manipulating her, deliberately feeding her sense of inadequacy to acquire and hold power over her.

In a healthy relationship, partners affirm the good things about each other. When a woman is feeling bad about herself, her partner is quick to point out her strengths and remind her of her positive qualities.

In an unhealthy relationship, an abusive and controlling partner only points out her weaknesses according to "his perception." Over time, he has convinced her that if she tries to stand up for herself, she is needy, selfish, and conceited. His continued berating warps her self-concept, draining her own Emotional Bank Account. Consequently, her self-talk becomes cruel and disparaging.

Since he's worked hard to isolate her from most of her friends and family, there are few people to refute the image he's painted of her. If he allows her family to remain in the picture, it is usually because he has conned them with his lies and smooth talk and turned them against her. Her support base now sides with him and sees her as the problem.

So saturated with his opinion, she loses her real self and gives up. She has become numb to the abuse and has stopped trusting her instincts, intelligence, and capabilities. Fear controls her life. She no longer remembers her personal goals and passions. To survive in this relationship that has become increasingly abusive, her total focus is on her partner and pleasing him—to be safe and to keep the children safe.

But as long as the relationship stays as is, neither she nor the children will ever be safe.

yes, but . . .

I Have No Choice

or

There's No Way Out

or

There's Nothing I Can Do

. . . .

I always have a choice. Not all choices are easy. Some choices may be between bad and worse. However, there is always something I can do. It may not be simple, or comfortable, and it may take some time, but there is a way out and there are people who will help guide me.

To grow strong enough to change the situation, I must first change myself, starting with my self-talk. It's time to stop telling myself that

~ *I'm stupid and will never be able to survive on my own*

~ *I can control this situation by my behavior*

~ *I deserve punishment*

~ *No one cares about me or will help me*

~ *He is powerful in the community and will win custody of my children*

~ *I can't care for my children on my own*

~ *I can't make it in the big, scary world without him*

~ *I'll be embarrassed when people know how I lived*

In my journal, I will note my self-defeating and disparaging thoughts and write healthy affirmations to replace them.

I'll take back my power and choose what is best for my children and me. I'll pay attention to what I tell myself and not allow the old messages in my head to frighten or prevent me from doing what I must do to protect us. I will

~ *do this at my own pace*

~ *take my focus off my partner and refocus on my children and myself*

~ *find a support group and/or therapist*

~ *call the National Domestic Violence Hotline for help: 800-799-SAFE (7233)*

~ *set up a safety plan—with the help of a therapist or the domestic violence center—that includes (1) identifying a safe place to go to in emergencies; (2) having clothing, money, and copies of important documents hidden with a friend; and (3) teaching the children where to go and what to do in an emergency (For more information, see Safety Planning on pages 207–211.)*

~ *accept help from my local service center to work with the legal system concerning protective orders and/or divorce proceedings*

I will model self-improvement and self-respect for my children.

In my journal, I'll develop a plan for moving forward.

TRUTHS

- I always have a choice.
- Not all choices are easy.
- I will change my self-talk.
- I am capable and can take care of myself (and my children).
- I will move at my own pace.
- I'll do what is best for my children and me.
- Modeling how to face pain and obstacles and deal with them is healthy for my children.

ISSUES TO EXPLORE

1. Safety planning
2. Recognizing and rewriting the old messages in my head
3. Fear of failure
4. Local available help

 *yes, but . . .*

No One Else Will Ever Love Me

or

This Is Better Than Being Alone

Allowing myself to believe these statements holds me in this relationship. My self-talk will now remind me that I am intelligent, capable, and worth loving.

My partner calls me worthless, stupid, and many other names to destroy my self-esteem. His goal is to make me feel helpless and powerless so I won't leave. I am neither helpless nor powerless. I refuse to believe his lies.

Though he tells me that no one else would want me, I know better. There's a good chance that I'll eventually meet someone who will love and respect me. First, I must learn to love and respect myself. Therapy or group work will help.

In truth, it's been hard work to maintain this relationship. If I refocus that energy and direct it toward healing, with time, other relationship opportunities will come. Who better to devote my energy to than my children and me?

I can work on the things that will enrich my life. I can develop my gifts and talents, skills I may have set aside during my relationship. As frightened as I am of failure, I'll direct my thoughts to where I'm going, plod through the fear, and keep my face pointed to my goal of emotional health. I'll build a good life for me and my children.

In my journal, I'll make a list of things that are worse than being alone. Here are some examples.

Being with someone who

~ *physically, emotionally, or sexually abuses me*

~ *mistreats our children*

~ *is concerned about only his own pleasure*

~ *is demanding*

~ *is demeaning*

~ *is not trustworthy*

~ *scares me*

If I stay in this relationship, I won't have the opportunity to find a new relationship. I'll be putting all my effort into maintaining peace—an impossible task.

I will not rush into a new relationship. Although I'd like to find a new partner someday, I must take the time needed to learn that I can take care of myself and heal the wounds from this relationship before seeking someone who could be my equal partner for this journey.

By not rushing into a new relationship, I'm demonstrating to my children that taking care of myself is important. Children learn what they live. If I show them how to set boundaries and make good decisions, they'll be more likely to create healthy lives for themselves. I'll give this gift to my children.

TRUTHS

- I'm intelligent, capable, and worth loving.
- I retain power over my own life.
- I will direct my energy into healing myself.
- I will learn to trust my inner voice and regain my self-respect.

- I will use the tools I learn in therapy to heal, taking the time I need to heal and allowing myself time before I seek a new relationship.
- I have to be healthy to attract a healthy partner.

ISSUES TO EXPLORE

1. Building self-esteem
2. Trusting my inner voice
3. Fear of not being in a relationship/learning to enjoy my own company

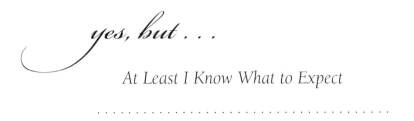

At Least I Know What to Expect

. . . .

Fear of the unknown is often the biggest barrier to taking the first step. I refuse to stay in a relationship just because it's what I know. Yes, I know what to expect but that includes being hurt, living in fear, and feeling demoralized.

I also refuse to stay just because I'm afraid I'll end up in a worse relationship. With professional guidance and some work, it's likely that I will end up in a better one.

A bad relationship is not better than being alone. Neither my children nor I can flourish in an abusive, stressful, and frightening atmosphere.

I expect to be with a partner who

> ~ *speaks kindly to me and the children*
> ~ *helps me when asked*
> ~ *encourages me when I try something new*
> ~ *is compassionate*
> ~ *listens to my opinion and respects it even if he doesn't agree*
> ~ *includes me in decisions that affect our family*
> ~ *keeps my confidences*
> ~ *shares his feelings*

TRUTHS

* A bad relationship is not better than being alone.
* I deserve love and respect.

ISSUES TO EXPLORE

1. Why I have been willing to put up with abuse
2. How I expect to be treated in a relationship
3. How to set clear expectations in relationships

At Least I'm Having Sex

. . . .

"Without the essential ingredient, the expression of love and affection, the sex act is totally devoid of primary benefits such as prolonged security and satisfaction; this can be achieved only in complete physical and emotional union. Like any drug, sex without love becomes simply an expression of basic physical need and personal desire and wears off as soon as orgasm is achieved, accomplishing nothing toward prolonged relating or loving."

LEO BUSCAGLIA, *LOVING EACH OTHER*

In my journal, or during a quiet moment, I'll consider these questions:

~ *Do my partner and I enter into a sexual encounter out of love and desire?*

~ *Do I feel filled or empty after sex?*

~ *Is my partner as concerned about my pleasure as I am about his?*

~ *Is there intimacy and trust in our sexual encounters?*

~ *Can I relax and trust that my partner will not hurt me during sex?*

~ *Can I trust that my partner will never force, threaten, or coerce me to participate in sexual acts that I find embarrassing, uncomfortable, or painful?*

~ *Does my partner get angry if I don't have an orgasm? (For more information on sexual abuse, see What Is Abuse? on page 197.)*

If I leave this relationship, I will eventually find a partner with whom I can enjoy great sex, someone who genuinely cares about me and my pleasure. Anyone can learn the mechanics, but sex that includes emotional closeness is the best. Because my partner is only concerned about his own pleasure, healthy sex will never be possible in this relationship.

Recognizing that sex is a major driving force in humans, I will not let my fear of being alone hold me in an unhealthy relationship.

TRUTHS

- Sex that includes emotional closeness is the best.
- My partner should be as concerned about my pleasure as he is about his own.
- It is healthy for partners to discuss their desires and expectations regarding sex.

ISSUES TO EXPLORE

1. What I consider to be a healthy sex life
2. The role of sex in my relationship

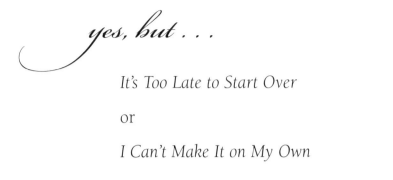

It's Too Late to Start Over

or

I Can't Make It on My Own

. . . .

Right now, I may be feeling old and worn. This relationship has turned off my inner light. With help and support, I can change that. I can once again look to the future with hope, excited about the opportunities that wait for me. When I start to work on myself, I'll find new energy and feel revived.

I'm not stuck. Regardless of my age, it is not too late for me to start again. I don't need to punish myself for not catching on to the games my partner played that enticed me into this relationship or for allowing it to continue for this long. The biggest mistake I can make is to live with abuse one day longer than I have to.

All my original gifts and abilities are still in me. I can develop them. I worked hard on this relationship. I'll refocus that energy into healing.

TRUTHS

- I am capable.
- With help and support, I can turn on my inner light again.
- My inner gifts are still with me and can be developed.

ISSUES TO EXPLORE

1. My new life plan
2. How to identify self-defeating thoughts and change them into self-enhancing thoughts

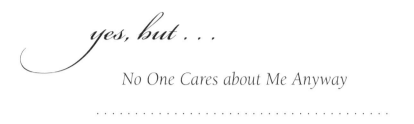

yes, but . . .

No One Cares about Me Anyway

. . . .

The most important person who needs to care about me is me. I must first love myself. I can take steps to achieve self-love and self-respect by developing an awareness of what I've been through and going to therapy or a support group.

I also have friends and family members who care about me. Those who are positive and encouraging will become my support system. I will let go of the others. As I move forward with my new life, my support network will naturally expand as I meet new people and participate in new activities.

TRUTHS

- The most important person who needs to care about me is me.
- Other people in my life care about me as well.
- I'll surround myself with supportive people.

ISSUES TO EXPLORE

1. How to better care for myself
2. People who are in my support system
3. How I can expand my support network

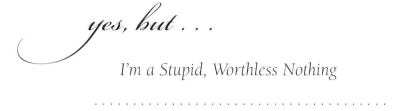

yes, but . . .

I'm a Stupid, Worthless Nothing

. . . .

My partner's actions toward me do not reflect my worth or value. His behavior is about the person he is—someone who is insecure, cruel, and selfish.

He's lying when he tells me I'm stupid and worthless. He tries to convince me that I'm crazy and can't make it in the world without him. He does all this in an effort to destroy my self-confidence so I'll stay with him. This is a power and control issue.

I won't buy into these lies anymore.

Everyone and everything has a place and purpose. Each person is born with gifts and talents that need to be developed. This includes me.

I'm an intelligent and capable person. Just like everyone else, I have areas that I excel in and others that I don't. That doesn't make me stupid; it makes me human. I'm much smarter than my partner believes—smart enough to know I don't deserve abuse.

TRUTHS

- I'll shed all hurtful labels.
- Everyone and everything has a place and purpose.

- I was born with gifts and talents and will work at developing them.
- I'm intelligent and capable.
- I'll encourage my children to find their gifts and talents.

ISSUES TO EXPLORE

1. Shedding the shame
2. Identifying harmful labels and discarding them
3. Learning how to develop positive coping strategies

I Am Embarrassed and Ashamed
to Be in This Situation

. . . .

It's hard to admit to myself, let alone others, how difficult and painful my life is right now, but if I want to move ahead, I must face this fact. I will not let my pride hold me in an unhealthy relationship. It's okay to tell others what our relationship has truly been like. His behavior is his shame, not mine. The only shame for me would be to continue in this relationship any longer than I have to.

People who love me want the best for me. They aren't judgmental. They'll want to emotionally support and encourage me.

TRUTHS

- This relationship *is* difficult and painful.
- My partner's behavior is his shame, not mine.
- My friends and family members who love me want the best for me.
- I'll protect my children and myself.
- I won't stay one day longer than I have to for my children's and my safety.

ISSUES TO EXPLORE

1. Shedding the shame
2. How to approach the subject with those whom I would like to tell, and how much I feel I can tell them

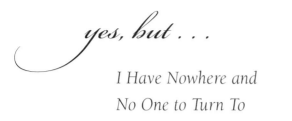

yes, but . . .

*I Have Nowhere and
No One to Turn To*

. . . .

Whatever happens, I'll get through it. Resources are available to lend a hand. A therapist or support group can help me, or I can call the domestic abuse hotline (see phone book for local listings). The staff will teach me how to set up a safety plan and help me leave when I'm ready. They will find a temporary safe place for my children and me, if needed, and walk me through any necessary legal processes. If there is no center near me, I will call the National Domestic Violence Hotline for help: 800-799-SAFE (7233).

It will take work, but I am up to the task. My children and I deserve a better life.

TRUTHS

- I can get help.
- I can find a safe place for my children and me.
- I am up to the task.
- My children and I deserve a peaceful life.

ISSUES TO EXPLORE

1. Local resources to help me
2. My safety plan

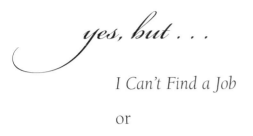

I Can't Find a Job

or

I Have No Skills

. . . .

I do have skills—life skills and abilities. Though I may not have earned a salary while I developed these skills, they are still valuable and can help me secure a job that will lead me to financial independence.

In my journal, I will list the life skills that would make me a valuable employee. Some examples include the following:

~ *Organized*

~ *Able to read people's body language*

~ *Perceptive*

~ *A peacemaker*

~ *Diplomatic*

~ *Resourceful*

~ *Wise with my time*

~ *Able to multitask*

If necessary, I can go to school to receive training for a job or to learn a profession.

TRUTHS

- I have life skills that will help me qualify for a job.
- I can learn.

ISSUES TO EXPLORE

1. Organizations to help me find a job
2. Educational opportunities

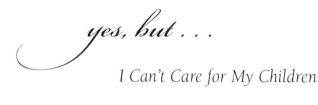

yes, but . . .

I Can't Care for My Children

. . . .

This is one of the many things my partner pummeled into my mind to frighten me so I wouldn't leave him. The truth is I *can* take care of my children. I have worked hard to protect them and maintain peace in our home. If I focus on caring for my children and myself, with the help of a therapist, the domestic abuse center, and state organizations, I can succeed.

TRUTHS

- I can care for my children.
- I am a capable parent, especially when I am free of the abuse.
- The time and attention I give my children will help them grow into self-confident and loving adults.

ISSUES TO EXPLORE

1. A plan to find a safe place for my children and me
2. Local organizations that will assist me

yes, but . . .

If I Try to Do Something, It May Backfire and Make the Situation Worse

. . . .

Doing something—whether it's taking a break, seeking support, leaving, or therapy—is better than living in the present situation. If I do nothing, the situation will likely grow more violent and could even result in my death. If I plan carefully for our safety, with the help of my therapist, domestic abuse organizations, and the police, I can bring my children and myself through this. (For more information on safety planning, see pages 207–211.)

TRUTHS

- Doing something is better than living with abuse.
- I will work with people who can protect and advise me.

ISSUES TO EXPLORE

1. Protection
2. Developing a safety plan

yes, but . . .

*Someone Else Will See What
He Is Doing and Save Me*

As much as I would like a knight in shining armor to rescue me or fix this relationship, it's not going to happen. I must be my own hero. It's my job to save myself. Others can help and support me, but I must make the decisions and carry the responsibility. This is the only way to take back the power and control in my life. Today I will begin by quieting the voice of fear my partner has instilled in me and trusting my authentic inner voice. I will reach out for help and expect the best.

TRUTHS

- It's my job to take action to change the situation.
- I can take back my power and control.
- My inner voice tells me the truth.

ISSUES TO EXPLORE

1. Learning to trust my instincts
2. Dealing with fear

Appendix A

EDUCATIONAL TOOLS

WHAT IS ABUSE?

PHYSICAL ABUSE

Physical abuse includes any physical interaction that causes you pain, injury, or restraint. If your partner engages in any of the following behaviors, this constitutes physical abuse:

- Slaps, hits, punches, or kicks you
- Abandons you in dangerous places
- Bites you
- Strangles you
- Forces you off the road
- Holds you to prevent you from leaving or moving
- Locks you out of the house or car
- Pushes or shoves you
- Refuses to help when you are sick, injured, or pregnant
- Threatens or burns you with an object or weapon
- Throws objects at you

EMOTIONAL ABUSE

- Is frequently jealous
- Continually criticizes you or calls you names
- Continually shouts or screams at you
- Controls your money
- Harasses you about relationships you've never had

- Humiliates you in private or public
- Ignores your feelings
- Insists on making decisions for you
- Insists that you did things you did not do in order to make you think you are crazy or incompetent
- Insults or drives away your family or friends
- Keeps you from working
- Manipulates you with lies and contradictions
- Punishes or deprives you when angry at you
- Refuses to socialize with you
- Refuses to work or share money
- Regularly threatens to leave you or tells you to leave
- Ridicules or insults women as a group
- Ridicules or insults your feelings, beliefs, religion, race, heritage, or class
- Takes or controls your car, money, or possessions
- Tells you about affairs in order to hurt you
- Threatens to hurt you or your family
- Threatens to hurt you if you leave or say you will leave
- Abuses pets to hurt you
- Withholds approval, appreciation, or affection as punishment

SPIRITUAL ABUSE

- Prevents you from attending worship
- Demeans your beliefs and practices of faith
- Forces you to do things against your beliefs
- Sets rigid rules
- Twists faith tenets to assert his power
- Expects prayer to cure all instead of taking action
- Is intolerant of varying opinions
- Is intolerant of others' errors

- Judges others harshly
- Considers himself spiritually superior to others
- Claims to be speaking for God
- Blames Satan instead of taking responsibility for his own behavior
- Is more concerned about the illusion of who the family is than the reality
- Gives time and money to the church at the expense of family needs
- Misuses a spiritual leadership role to coerce or manipulate parishioners and/or intimidate you

SEXUAL ABUSE

- Calls you derogatory sexual names
- Rapes you by doing one or more of the following:
  - Forces sex
  - Forces sex when you are sick or when sex is a danger to your health
  - Forces you to have sex with others
  - Forces unwanted sexual acts
  - Drugs you in order to have sex
  - Has sex with you when you are drunk and unable to give consent
- Forces you to strip against your will
- Forces you to watch him or others have sex
- Has affairs with other people after agreeing to maintain a monogamous relationship with you
- Insists or forces you to dress in a more sexual way than you want
- Becomes jealous, angry, or accusing, assuming that you would have sex with other people
- Publicly shows sexual interest in other people
- Tells anti-woman jokes, or makes demeaning remarks about your gender
- Withholds sex and affection

PROFILE OF AN ABUSER

The following lists of general characteristics and behaviors of abusers can help you evaluate what's happening in your relationship. Abusers vary in the style and severity of abuse they inflict. These lists will help you evaluate whether you are in a dangerous relationship or just have a few issues to resolve. Check the statements that relate to your situation.

If you mark only a few behaviors that are disrespectful but non-life-threatening, you may be able to stop the unwanted behavior by addressing it and declaring that you will no longer tolerate it. It's important to remember not to set a consequence on which you are not willing to act. If you say you will leave if the behavior doesn't stop, be prepared to leave and not return. Hollow promises will only strengthen your partner's belief that he can treat you any way he pleases. If you are afraid even to broach the subject with your partner because he may become angry, you already have your answer. You are in an unhealthy relationship.

Some of the behaviors listed put your life at risk. If you check any physical attacks, you are in a very dangerous situation. Also, remember that verbal abuse is often a precursor to physical attacks.

JEALOUS AND POSSESSIVE

☐ Discourages or forbids me from seeing my friends or family
☐ Wants to know where I am at all times
☐ Wants to be with me all the time

CONTROLLING

☐ Prevents me from working

☐ Controls the money

☐ Chooses all activities

☐ Discourages or forbids me from attending worship services

☐ Forces me to attend his choice of worship services

☐ Uses my faith tenets to support his wants

LACK OF TRUST

☐ Shows up unexpectedly

☐ Calls to check up on me

☐ Accuses me of flirting or having affairs

EXPLOSIVE TEMPER AND/
OR LOSES CONTROL

☐ Slaps, hits, punches, or kicks me

☐ Screams

☐ Restrains me

☐ Throws things

☐ Punches, kicks, or knocks holes in walls

☐ Brandishes a weapon

ALWAYS PUTS HIS WANTS AND NEEDS
AHEAD OF MY WANTS AND NEEDS

☐ Expects me to wait for him no matter how long he takes

☐ Expects me to anticipate his every need

☐ Pressures me into sex

☐ Expects sex every time I see him

☐ Hurts me during sex

☐ Pressures me into doing sexual things that are uncomfortable or embarrassing

☐ Rarely satisfies me sexually

EMOTIONALLY ABUSIVE

☐ Tells me what I think and feel
☐ Tells me how I measure up against his former partners
☐ Treats me differently in front of his friends
☐ Ogles other women and comments about them in front of me '
☐ Threatens to commit suicide if I leave him
☐ Threatens to kill me and/or the children if I leave him

VERBALLY ABUSIVE

☐ Belittles me "for my own good"
☐ Criticizes my looks or behavior
☐ Tells me I'm stupid and worthless

MACHO

☐ Draws definite roles between men and women
☐ Makes rigid rules
☐ Cracks jokes that degrade others

COMES FROM A FAMILY THAT CONTAINED VIOLENCE

☐ Father was abusive to family members
☐ Mother was abusive to family members

BLAMES OTHER PEOPLE OR CIRCUMSTANCES FOR HIS BEHAVIOR

☐ Tells me I make him angry
☐ Tells me he's under stress
☐ Blames the alcohol or other drugs
☐ Projects his faults on me

DENIES BEHAVIOR OR
SEVERITY OF BEHAVIOR

☐ Tells me I'm overreacting

☐ Tells me he was just joking

☐ Tells me I'm too sensitive or to lighten up

DOES WHATEVER IT WILL TAKE TO GET ME BACK
AND KEEP ME IN THE RELATIONSHIP

☐ Cries and begs forgiveness—then returns to old behaviors

☐ Threatens to commit suicide

☐ Sends flowers or gifts

☐ Promises to quit drinking/doing drugs—then starts again

☐ Promises to control his anger—but doesn't

☐ Attends counseling—but quits after a few visits, using some weak excuse

☐ Pays more attention to me and the children—for a short time

CYCLE OF ABUSE

Abuse is not random. It occurs within a system of behaviors designed to maintain control. There are three distinct phases in the cycle.

Honeymoon Period

After the abuse, the perpetrator often becomes loving and contrite. He begs for forgiveness and promises it will never happen again. He promises to give up alcohol or other drugs and may agree to go into therapy. He says and does whatever is necessary to keep the victim in the relationship.

Serious Battering Incident

Any event, internal or external, can cause an explosion of verbal and/or physical battering. The perpetrator blames the victim to justify his behavior. He will both minimize and rationalize the event.

Tension-Building Period

When he feels his victim has been placated, he begins to revert to former behavior. He uses verbal and psychological abuse, denies or minimizes what happened, and does not take responsibility for his inappropriate behavior. He becomes more possessive and jealous. He is often angry for the effort he had to expend to keep her in the relationship.

The victim often believes the person her partner is during the honeymoon period is the "real" person. She may deny, explain away, and take responsibility for his behavior during the tension period.

This cycle is not a circle. Rather, it is a spiral. Over time, the battering occurs more frequently and the intensity increases. If not disrupted, the cycle may ultimately result in death for the victim.

CHART OF COERCION

METHOD OF ABUSE	EXAMPLES	EFFECT	PURPOSE
Isolates	Controls who you can talk to, where you go; limits contact with family, friends	Deprivation of social support; increased dependency on controller	Weaken the spirit and the ability to resist
Monopolizes Perception	Puts down what you want or think; disrupts your plans; focuses on own feelings/problems; blames you for everything	Reduction of competing stimuli; frustration of non-compliant actions	Instill confusion and self-doubt
Employs Constant Tension and Chaos	Applies constant pressure for compliance; delivers a barrage of verbal abuse; changes expectations without warning	Hyper-vigilance for signs of displeasure; fear, anxiety; despair; exhaustion	Teach that resisting is more difficult than complying
Threatens	Threatens to harm you, himself, pets, children, objects; threatens to report you or humiliate you; takes things away from you	Anxiety; fear; despair; hyper-vigilance	Assure reluctance to reach out for resources to help

METHOD OF ABUSE	EXAMPLES	EFFECT	PURPOSE
Demonstrates Omnipotence or Power	Controls money, access to knowledge, access to people; flaunts the law by suggesting he or she is above it; expects you to know everything; changes the rules each time	Inferiority; vulnerability; confusion	Instill a sense that resistance is futile
Humiliates and Degrades	Embarrasses you in public; devalues everything you do; uses sex or degrading acts to hurt and control you	Shame; focus on basic survival	Teach that resistance is more risky to self-esteem than compliance
Enforces Trivial Demands	Applies constant pressure or abuse until you give in; creates petty rules	Hyper-vigilance	Instill compliance habit
Indulges on Occasion	Surprises you with considerate behavior or gifts; responds indulgently when usually there is an abusive response	Confusion; hope for change	Reinforce positive motivation for compliance, encourage commitment to relationship

Reproduced by permission of Jennifer Parker, MSSW, 1998; adapted from *Getting Free*, Ginny NiCarthy, & The Safety Net, newslt. Published by Network for Women's Lives, 1997.

SAFETY PLANNING

Domestic abuse experts recommend that women in abusive relationships develop a safety plan if they are still living with an abuser and are planning to leave, or if they have already done so. The plan should cover all areas of their lives where the potential for abuse exists—including life at home, work, and in transit.

The list that follows provides some general considerations as you make your own safety plan; please use it as a starting point. Your local women's shelter, support group, or therapist may have guidelines as well.

1. **Make a list of names and places, including phone numbers, where you can go for help (friends, relatives, women's shelter, hospitals, houses of worship).**

    - Find a safe place to hide the list (at your neighbor's house, in the freezer, in a tampon box).
    - Post emergency numbers, such as police and fire station, by your phone.
    - Memorize important numbers.

2. **Keep all house and car keys out of sight.**

    - Give extra house and car keys to neighbors, friends, and relatives you trust.
    - Hide extra keys somewhere safe outside of the house.

3. **Protect your car from being immobilized.**

    - If able, collect abuser's set of keys to your vehicle.

- Get a lock for the hood and gas cap.
- If the hood can only be opened from inside the car, keep the doors locked at all times.
- Park your car where the abuser will not look for it.
- If you need glasses for driving, keep an extra pair in the car.

4. **Make your home safer.**
   - Change the locks on your house (if you have separated and your partner has a key).
   - Install locks on doors and windows.
   - Reinforce and repair any damaged windows and doors.
   - Obtain an alarm or a dog.
   - Move to another residence.
   - Install a peephole in your door.
   - Never let the abuser into your residence.
   - Install outdoor motion detection lights.

5. **Inform neighbors, friends, and relatives of the abuse.**
   - Give friends, neighbors, and relatives permission to call the police if they hear an altercation or see the abuser near you after you've obtained an order of protection.
   - Set up signals with friends and family asking for help when in danger. These may include the following:
     – Flicking lights on and off
     – Having a password sentence that indicates something isn't normal
     – Opening or shutting a curtain in a certain window
     – Taking down a plant that usually hangs in a certain window
     – Screaming "fire"
     – Knocking on walls to neighbor's apartment
   - Do not give information to untrustworthy people or people who like and trust the abuser.
   - Talk with your neighbors and friends and ask if you can come to them in the middle of the night.

6. Have a telephone.

- If you don't have a telephone, get one.
- Ask your local women's shelter if they have safety cell phones—they can be used only to dial 911.
- Change your phone number and make it unlisted.
- Get caller ID or an answering machine to screen calls.
- Refuse to argue on the telephone.
- Document your phone calls (it is legal to tape your own phone conversations).
- Hide a cell phone in your home.

7. Put aside some money for emergencies.

- Open a personal account separate from the abuser's at a different bank. Have all bank mail sent to a friend's house or post office box.
- When purchasing groceries or other items, write the check for over the amount and put that money in your personal account.
- Ask friends or relatives if they are willing to contribute some money to this account.
- Sell silver, jewelry, or other items for cash if you are able.
- Hide some cash and traveler's checks where they will be accessible to you in an emergency.
- Get a credit card just for emergencies, if possible.

8. Keep important papers and documents prepared in case you must leave in a hurry.

- Keep important papers in a safe place. Some such places include the following:
  - Safety deposit box at your personal bank
  - With friends or relatives
  - In the freezer
  - In a rented locker at the YMCA or bus station
- Such documents include birth certificates, marriage license, divorce

decree, social security card, insurance policies, bank papers, stock accounts, bank mortgages, car title, paycheck stubs, driver's license, and so on.

- Always carry your restraining order with you.

9. **Protect your children.**

- Explain to your children what is happening (even small children are affected by abuse and need to know what's going on and what they should do if they see abuse or the abuser).

- Inform your babysitter, schools, medical facilities, and parents of your child's friends that the child should not leave with the abuser.

- Don't allow your children to go to the homes of people you suspect are sympathetic to the abuser (even if this includes your child's best friend).

- Teach your children how to call the police; have a secret signal to tell them when.

- Develop a safety plan to use when they are scared or when you give them the signal (that is, where to hide, when and how to leave, and where to go for help).

10. **Protect your children and yourself from the abuser's weapons.**

- Hide or throw away all ammunition.

- Hide weapons or lock them away in the trunk of a car to which the abuser doesn't have a key.

- Put knives in inaccessible places.

- If law enforcement is called, ask them to remove the weapon from your home.

11. **Plan ahead.**

- Always be aware of your surroundings.

- Know good places in your house to hide (close to windows and doors for easy escape).

- Make an escape plan from each room in your home (hide rope ladders in upstairs rooms).

- Make a "safe" room that has a lock on the door, a phone, and a way you can escape from the house.
- Do not lock yourself into a small space such as a car or in a room with only one exit.
- Be aware of your physical capabilities. For example, can you out-run your abuser?
- If you are unable to drive away, lock yourself in a stranger's car rather than your own.
- Don't count on a stranger's help.
- Know in advance where you will go if you need to leave your house.

12. **Protect yourself before and during an assault.**
- Be aware of the abuser's cues before the assault (physical behaviors, circumstances). Try to leave before the assault.
- Find a self-defense class in your area. Check it out; if it feels safe and fulfills your needs, take it.
- Know ahead of time what you are capable of doing to defend yourself (for example, gouging eyes, kicking or kneeing crotch, or running).
- Keep your car keys with you at all times (and within reach at night); set off your car alarm if you need help.
- Never pick up a weapon unless you are sure you will use it (remember, if you become afraid to use it, the abuser might take it and use it on you).
- Throw or spray black pepper, chili powder, salt, or hairspray in the eyes of the abuser; these all can be effective ways to buy time when under attack.
- If all else fails, roll up in a ball and protect your head.

Appendix B

ADDITIONAL RESOURCES

HOTLINES AND WEB SITES

The following national resources provide information and can direct you to help in your local area. Please also consult your local phone books (look under "Domestic Abuse") for resources close to home.

DOMESTIC VIOLENCE

National Domestic Violence Hotline
Phone: 800-799-SAFE (7233)
Web site: www.ndvh.org

This organization runs a twenty-four-hour hotline that provides crisis intervention, safety planning, information, and local referrals. In addition, the Web site provides resources and educational material on domestic violence.

National Coalition Against Domestic Violence
Web site: www.ncadv.org

This site includes fact sheets, a list of state coalitions, and a suggested reading list.

Pennsylvania Coalition Against Domestic Violence
Phone: 800-537-2238 (office); 800-932-4632 (for information on your local domestic violence program)
Web site: www.pcadv.org

This organization is the nation's first state domestic violence coalition and works on the state and national levels to eliminate domestic violence.

U.S. Department of Agriculture
Safety, Health and Employee Welfare Division
Web site: www.da.usda.gov/shmd/aware.htm

This site provides a domestic violence awareness handbook and provides a list of additional Web resources.

National Child Traumatic Stress Network
Web site: www.nctsnet.org

This site provides information and resources on child traumatic stress (CTS).

RAVE: Religion and Violence e-Learning
Web site: www.theraveproject.org

This site provides information to religious leaders to help them respond to domestic violence in a "compassionate, practical, and informed" way. Some features of the site include FAQs, online training, and a listing of a wide variety of resources that religious staff can use when dealing with persons involved in domestic violence. For victims who are using the Internet to obtain information, RAVE has instructions on how to delete your surfing history from your computer. This site also includes stories from other victims.

LEGAL

American Bar Association
Web site: www.abanet.org/domviol/home.html

This site provides resources for attorneys dealing with domestic violence cases as well as links for victims of abuse who are looking for legal help.

TREATMENT FOR BATTERERS

Batterer Intervention Services Coalition Michigan
Treatment Standards across the U.S.
Web site: www.biscmi.org/other_resources/state_standards.html

This site provides information on individual state standards for batterer intervention programs.

RECOMMENDED READINGS

VIOLENCE

Emotional Blackmail: When the People in Your Life Use Fear, Obligation, and Guilt to Manipulate You by Susan Forward, Harper Paperbacks, New York, 1998

Getting Free: You Can End Abuse and Take Back Your Life by Ginny NiCarthy, Seal Press, Berkley, CA, 2004

I Hate You—Don't Leave Me: Understanding the Borderline Personality by Jerold J. Kreisman and Hal Straus, Avon, New York, 1991

Living with the Passive-Aggressive Man by Scott Wetzler, Fireside, New York, 1993

Men Who Hate Women and the Women Who Love Them: When Loving Hurts and You Don't Know Why by Susan Forward, Bantam Books, New York, 2002

No Place for Abuse: Biblical and Practical Resources to Counteract Domestic Violence by Catherine Clark Kroeger and Nancy Nason-Clark, InterVarsity Press, Downers Grove, IL, 2001

The Verbally Abusive Relationship: How to Recognize It and How to Respond by Patricia Evans, Adams Media, Cincinnati, OH, 2003

When Love Goes Wrong: What to Do When You Can't Do Anything Right by Ann Jones and Susan Schechter, Harper Paperbacks, New York, 1993

Why Does He Do That? Inside the Minds of Angry and Controlling Men by Lundy Bancroft, Berkley Books, New York, 2003

CODEPENDENCY

Anxious to Please: 7 Revolutionary Practices for the Chronically Nice by James Rapson and Craig English, Sourcebooks, Naperville, IL, 2006

Codependent No More: How to Stop Controlling Others and Start Caring for Yourself by Melody Beattie, Hazelden, Center City, MN, 1992

The Dance of Anger: A Woman's Guide to Changing the Patterns of Intimate Relationships by Harriet Lerner, Harper Paperbacks, New York, 2005

Do I Have to Give Up Me to Be Loved by You? by Jordan Paul and Margaret Paul, Hazelden, Center City, MN, 2002

The Feeling Good Handbook by David D. Burns, Plume, New York, 1999

EMOTIONAL AND SPIRITUAL HEALING

Forgiveness Is a Choice: A Step-by-Step Process for Resolving Anger and Restoring Hope by Robert D. Enright, APA LifeTools, Washington, DC, 2001

The Four Agreements: A Practical Guide to Personal Freedom, A Toltec Wisdom Book by Don Miguel Ruiz, Amber-Allen Publishing, San Rafael, CA, 1997

Friedman's Fables by Edwin H. Friedman, Guilford Press, New York, 1990

How Good Do We Have to Be? A New Understanding of Guilt and Forgiveness by Harold S. Kushner, Back Bay Books, New York, 1997

The Language of Love: How to Be Instantly Understood by Those You Love by Gary Smalley and John Trent, Tyndale House Publishers/Living Books, Carol Stream, IL, 2006

Life Strategies: Doing What Works, Doing What Matters by Phillip C. McGraw, Hyperion, New York, 1999

Living a Life That Matters by Harold S. Kushner, Anchor Books, New York, 2002

Loving Each Other: The Challenge of Human Relationships by Leo F. Buscaglia, Ballantine Books, New York, 1986

Rebuilding: When Your Relationship Ends by Bruce Fisher and Robert Alberti, Impact Publishers, Atascadero, CA, 2005

Self Matters: Creating Your Life from the Inside Out by Phillip C. McGraw, Simon & Schuster/Free Press, New York, 2001

The Seven Habits of Highly Effective People: Powerful Lessons in Personal Change by Stephen R. Covey, Simon & Schuster/Free Press, New York, 2004

Struggle for Intimacy by Janet Geringer Woititz, Health Communications, Deerfield Beach, FL, 1986

Toxic Faith: Understanding and Overcoming Religious Addiction by Stephen Arterburn and Jack Felton, Shaw Books, Colorado Springs, CO, 2001

Transitions: Making Sense of Life's Changes by William Bridges, Da Capo Press, Cambridge, MA, 2004

Women Who Run with the Wolves: Myths and Stories of the Wild Woman Archetype by Clarissa Pinkola Estés, Ballatine Books, New York, 1996

Women's Bodies, Women's Wisdom: Creating Physical and Emotional Health and Healing by Christiane Northrup, Bantam Books, New York, 2006

Your Perfect Right: Assertiveness and Equality in Your Life and Relationships by Robert E. Alberti and Michael L. Emmons, Impact Publishers, Atascadero, 2008

CHILDREN'S ISSUES

Children

The Batterer as Parent: Addressing the Impact of Domestic Violence on Family Dynamics by Lundy Bancroft and Jay G. Silverman, Sage Publications, Thousand Oaks, CA, 2002

Childhood Experiences of Domestic Violence by Caroline McGee, Jessica Kingsley Publishers, London, 2009

Children Who See Too Much: Lessons from the Child Witness to Violence Project by Betsy McAlister Groves, Beacon Press, Boston, 2003

Learning to Listen, Learning to Help: Understanding Woman Abuse and Its Effects on Children by Linda Baker and Alison Cunningham, Centre for Children and Families in the Justice System, London Family Court Clinic, London, Ontario, 2005. Available as free download at www.lfcc.on.ca/learning.html.

Little Eyes, Little Ears: How Violence Against a Mother Shapes Children as They Grow by Alison Cunningham and Linda Baker, Centre for Children and Families in the Justice System, London Family Court Clinic, London, Ontario, 2007. Available as free download at www.lfcc.on.ca/little_eyes_little_ears.html.

Teens

The Breakable Vow by Kathryn Ann Clarke, HarperCollins, New York, 2004. Fiction book, written for teens

But I Love Him: Protecting Your Teen Daughter from Controlling, Abusive Dating Relationships by Jill Murray, HarperCollins, New York, 2001

NOTES

1. Minnesota Advocates for Human Rights, "Cause and Theories of Domestic Violence," Stop Violence Against Women: A Project by the Advocates for Human Rights, www.stopvaw.org/sites/3f6d15f4-c12d-4515-8544-26b7a3a5a41e/uploads/TheoriesDV.PDF.

2. Larry W. Bennett, "Myths about Alcohol and Domestic Violence," Stop Violence Against Women: A Project by the Advocates for Human Rights, www.stopvaw.org/Myths_About_Alcohol_and_Domestic_Violence.html.

3. "Intimate Partner Violence in the U.S.," U.S. Department of Justice, Bureau of Justice Statistics, December 2006, www.ojp.usdoj.gov/bjs/intimate/victims.htm.

4. A Safe Place: Lake County Crisis Center, "Statistics of Battered Women," www.asafeplaceforhelp.org/batteredwomenstatistics.html.

5. "Intimate Partner Violence in the U.S.: Victim Characteristics, 1976–2005," U.S. Department of Justice, Bureau of Justice Statistics, www.ojp.usdoj.gov/bjs/intimate/victims.htm.

6. "Homicide Trends in the U.S.: Intimate Homicide," U.S. Department of Justice, Bureau of Justice Statistics, www.ojp.usdoj.gov/bjs/homicide/intimates.htm.

7. Leo Buscaglia, *Loving Each Other: The Challenge of Human Relationships* (New York: Ballantine Books, 1986), 15.

8. V. Frye, "Examining Homicide's Contribution to Pregnancy-Associated Deaths," *Journal of the American Medical Association* 285, no. 11 (2001).

9. Lundy Bancroft, *Why Does He Do That? Inside the Minds of Angry and Controlling Men* (New York: Berkley Books, 2003), 19.

10. Callie Marie Rennison, "Intimate Partner Violence, 1993–2001," *Bureau of Justice Statistics Crime Data Brief* (February 2003).

11. Bessel van der Kolk, "The Body Keeps the Score: Memory and the Evolving Psychobiology of Post Traumatic Stress," *Harvard Review of Psychiatry* 1, no. 5 (1994): 253–65.

12. The Stockholm Syndrome describes the behavior of kidnapping victims who, over time, become sympathetic to their captors. The name comes from a hostage incident in Stockholm, Sweden, in 1973. After six days of captivity in a bank, several kidnapping victims resisted rescue attempts and later refused to testify against their captors.

13. 2 Timothy 1:7.

14. See *Why Does He Do That?* or *The Batterer as a Parent* by Lundy Bancroft for a better understanding of this complicated topic.

15. Stephen R. Covey, *The Seven Habits of Highly Effective People: Powerful Lessons in Personal Change* (New York: Simon & Schuster, 2004), 188.

16. Bill Moyers Journal, *Beyond Our Differences,* DVD, directed by Peter Bisanz (Alexandria, VA: PBS Home Video, 2009).

17. "Toxic faith is a destructive and dangerous relationship with a religion that allows the religion, not the relationship with God, to control a person's life." Definition is from the following: Stephen Arterburn and Jack Felton, *Toxic Faith: Understanding and Overcoming Religious Addiction* (Nashville, TN: Thomas Nelson, 1991), 31.

18. The phrase *Emotional Bank Account* is from the following: Stephen R. Covey, *The Seven Habits of Highly Successful People: Powerful Lessons in Personal Change* (New York: Simon & Schuster/Free Press, 2004), 188.

19. TED: The Editor's Desk, "Women's Earnings as a Percentage of Men's, 1979–2007, U.S. Department of Labor, Bureau of Labor Statistics, October 29, 2008, www.bls.gov/opub/ted/2008/oct/wk4/art03.htm.